First
Thing
Monday
Morning

DIANNA BOOHER

First Thing Monday Morning

Fleming H. Revell
Old Tappan, New Jersey

LIBRARY OF CONGRESS
Library of Congress Cataloging-in-Publication Data

Booher, Dianna Daniels
 First thing Monday morning / Dianna Booher.
    p.   cm.
 ISBN 0-8007-1595-0
 1. Christian life—Humor.   2. Business—Religious aspects—
Christianity—Humor.   I. Title.
BV4517.B66 1988
248.4—dc19   88-10330
                                                         CIP

Copyright © 1988 by Dianna Booher
Published by the Fleming H. Revell Company
Old Tappan, New Jersey 07675
Printed in the United States of America

In memory of my grandparents,
Albert and Anna Schronk
and
Allen and Mabel Daniels

And, once again, to my parents,
Alton and Opal Daniels

All of whom taught and lived
most of the truths on these pages

Contents

Introduction

"Stocks plummet. Harrison wins the mayor's race. The storms continue with major flooding in the area. Stay tuned for details at ten."

And so goes the nightly TV news commentator with weather and business briefs for harried and hurried business people. We get so accustomed to the pace—fast foods, fast cars, overnight mail, one-day printing, and two-hour laundry service—that sometimes we have little time and energy left for God. Particularly, between eight and five.

A century ago, gathering the family around the table for Bible reading was not an unfamiliar scene. Today it is. Frequently the Bible is the last thing we include in our reading schedule sometime after the newspaper, mail, magazine, professional journal, and file notes for tomorrow's meeting.

But approaching our work environment without hearing God's voice can be as disappointing, even disastrous, as striking out on vacation without being briefed on the weather reports for our destination. Every time I read through Proverbs particularly, I become more aware just how practical—and essential—the Bible is for everyday business situations.

First Thing Monday Morning focuses attention on what God might be saying to us if He briefed us weekly about bringing our Christianity to the office.

Whether you're an employee or employer, I hope these fifty-two business briefs help you start each week with God's measure of success.

Dianna Booher

First Thing
Thing
Monday
Morning

1. Humor in the Boardroom

A merry heart doeth good like a medicine: but a broken spirit drieth the bones.

Proverbs 17:22

People show their character and their Christianity by what they think is funny. And sooner or later, we must deal with all forms of humor popping up in the workplace: repartee, wit, irony, cynicism, jokes, pranks, and ridicule. Most of us can quote the first half of the above proverb, but we have not often placed equal emphasis on the last portion. Humor can build people up or knock them down, ease tension or create hostility, make a heavy disagreement lighter or make a minor conflict unbearable, attract people to our faith or cause them to run from righteousness.

A sense of humor can be sunshine in a windowless office or a reward during an economic downturn. First of all, it helps us step back from the seriousness of a situation and put difficulties into perspective. Eleanor Roosevelt once observed that without the ability to treat serious things lightly after the heavy thinking is done and the decisions reached, no person could long carry out the job of president of the United States.

President Reagan's humor has done more to calm the minds of American citizens than a flood of official press releases. First, there was the comment as he was wheeled into surgery after being shot by a would-be assassin in 1981. To the doctors about to perform surgery, he quipped, "I hope you're all Republicans."

A few years later in the debates with presidential contender Walter Mondale, seventy-three-year-old Reagan was questioned about his age and his ability to lead the nation in a second term. "I will not make age an issue in this campaign," he replied. "I am not going to exploit for political reasons my opponent's youth and inexperience."

In a 1985 meeting with Mikhail Gorbachev in Switzerland, Reagan temporarily put the destiny of the entire world aside to tell the Soviet leader a light story: A Russian and an American are discussing how their nations differ. The American says, "I can walk into Reagan's office, slam my fist down on his desk, and tell him I don't like the way he's running the country." The Russian pauses and then replies, "But I can do the same thing in the Soviet Union. I can walk into the Politburo, slam my fist down on Gorbachev's desk, and say, 'I don't like the way Reagan is running the United States.' "

Humor also serves its purpose when it permits us to be children again, to step outside the pressure of the adult role of always having the answers and handling the problems correctly. We can laugh for a few minutes and postpone the tears involved in solving a problem confronting us. A family was called into the office of the school superintendent to discuss what should be done about their son, who had been caught selling marijuana to his schoolmates. Although he had a broken heart and every intention of doing whatever it took to solve the problem, the father was able to step out of his adult role as problem solver for a brief moment through his sense of humor: "Well, obviously this kid's a born salesman; all we've got to do is find him a better product."

Humor can be a powerful tension reliever, especially the kind of humor that brings a belly laugh. When people with potential conflicts are thrown into a situation together, the joking relationship that results often permits them to relax in an environment where everyone agrees not to take offense.

Another benefit of humor is that it creates bonds between people. When two people allude to something with a knowing wink and smile, informing other listeners, "That's an old joke," they draw a circle around themselves. This line often says, "We've been through the fire together and have shuffled something into a solution, or at least into perspective." Humor often brings believers into emotional intimacy.

Self-deprecatory humor can help us rise above feelings of inferiority. A popular notion says if we can laugh at ourselves before others do, we're well-adjusted people. We cast a protective shell around our shoulders so another's criticism doesn't hurt so much.

Even positive physical benefits can come from a good strong laugh. Laughter can relieve headaches and lower blood pressure. On some of the TV commercials with before-and-after headache sufferers, I often wonder if the cured person's smile came before or after the headache left. Which was the cause and which the effect? It would be cheaper and quicker to listen to a child's laughter than to reach into the medicine cabinet.

Finally, a sense of humor attracts others to God in our lives. Seventeenth-century Protestant clergyman James Usher observed: "If good people would but make their goodness agreeable, and smile instead of frowning in their virtue, how many would they win to the good cause." A good sense of humor may be the most important thing to wear when you go out in public.

But for all the positive attractions of humor, Christians should be wary of its ambiguous nature. People use humor to probe for another's values and interests when they're not sure how the listener feels. For example, if someone tells a racist or lewd joke and the listener joins in the laughter, the joke teller assumes the listener shares his devaluation of women, sex, or an entire race. If the listener doesn't respond to the would-be humor, the teller knows he's on dangerous ground and can back down on the topic without an outright declaration of his attitudes or values.

As far as our Christian witness goes, then, what we don't laugh at may be as important as what we do laugh at. The English author Izaak Walton had the right perspective when he said, "I love such mirth as does not make friends ashamed to look upon one another next morning."

We also should not overlook the last portion of the proverb: "a broken spirit drieth the bones."

Humor should spread a smile, not wrinkle a brow. We may use self-deprecating wit on ourselves as a shield of self-defense, but we should never use sarcasm as a sword to wound others. About civil rights issues and personal freedom, we've often heard the cliché: Your freedom to swing your arm ends where my nose begins. Where humor is concerned, your freedom to benefit from humor ends where another's broken spirit begins.

But office humor doesn't always show up where you expect it—out on the assembly line or at the telephone switchboard. Rather, sociologist Rose Laub Coser, who did a study of the uses of humor among the staff of a mental hospital, found that humor almost always flows downward. That is, those higher up in the organizational hierarchy make jokes at the expense of those workers beneath them. Office humor may be our way of supporting the social structure; we laugh at others' expense because we want to feel superior.

Does all this mean that we should check our sense of humor at the boardroom door? Of course not.

There are those of us who laugh too much and those who laugh too little. We can use our sense of humor to attract others to our faith or to repel them with our reserve and pride. We as Christians should be as purposeful and as careful with our humor as with our checkbook.

For Further Reflection:

Being happy-go-lucky around a person whose heart is heavy is as bad as stealing his jacket in cold weather, or rubbing salt in his wounds.

Proverbs 25:20 TLB

Laughter cannot mask a heavy heart. When the laughter ends, the grief remains.

Proverbs 14:13 TLB

2. Failure— And Not Yet Forty

My heart throbs, my strength fails me; and the light of my eyes—it also has gone from me. My friends and companions stand aloof from my plague, and my kinsmen stand afar off.

Psalms 38:10 RSV

Hear me speedily, O Lord; my spirit faileth: hide not thy face from me, lest I be like unto them that go down into the pit. Cause me to hear thy lovingkindness in the morning; for in thee do I trust: cause me to know the way wherein I should walk; for I lift up my soul unto thee.

Psalms 143:7, 8

Sylvester Stallone's income per movie has reached $16 million. The average major-league baseball player earns $412,520 each year. The president's annual salary is $200,000. The pope has no salary at all.

Although many give lip service to the idea that success can't be measured in dollars and cents, in the business world, one seems to foreshadow the other. That is, income—or the lack thereof—often becomes the yardstick for success or failure.

Rare is the employee who has never compared his or her bank account to that of another individual: "If I'd been as sharp as Joe, I'd have developed that idea and started a business like his." Or, "If I'd finished earning that degree, I'd be a little more eager to go to that class reunion."

Agreeing wholeheartedly that money doesn't necessarily equal success, most of us nevertheless feel like failures from time to time. We forget that success is not external; it's internal.

If it's not the size of our paycheck that brings on that gnawing desperation, it may be continual put-downs from the boss. It may be a failure in marriage or in other family relationships or friendships. It may be failure in overcoming a personal habit. It may be failure caused by poor health. Whatever the reason, let's consider the feeling of failure more closely.

Proverbs 14:23 tells us that in all work (even failure) there is profit. If you've ever spent $50,000 manufacturing a product nobody wants to buy, you know that verse has to be referring to something other than money as profit!

So what's the profit? With the right thought process, we can psychologically prepare not to repeat our failures. Physiologist Robert Pozos of the University of Minnesota in Duluth has shown, for example, that a person who falls into frigid water but remains calm will suffer a slower drop in core temperature than one who panics. Studies by Niels Birbaumer of Pennsylvania State University have shown that patients can even raise the temperature of their hands and feet by using mental imagery, such as imagining they are touching hot coals. Birbaumer notes that apparently the part of the brain that controls higher thought can actually change the activity of the hypothalamus (*Newsweek*, March 9, 1987).

If we as humans can think ourselves out of being cold or freezing to death, surely we can think ourselves out of failure! Failure can be profit; it teaches us the following lessons:

We Can't Please Everyone

Comedian Bill Cosby says, "I don't know the key to success, but the key to failure is trying to please everybody." Many people wake up in mid-life to find they have spent all their energy trying to please a spouse, a parent, a friend, or a boss. Job, the Old Testament man of God, certainly knew what it was to stand against what his family and friends tried to tell him was wrong with his life. Listening to them was like listening to a daily litany of failure.

We rarely feel successful when we let everybody else put his or her thumb on our measuring scale. Remember that God will be the final judge of how we've spent our days.

We Learn to Take Risks

Around the jogging track, we comfort each other with, "No pain, no gain." In the corporate world, it's, "No risks, no payback." We have to invest money, time, or effort in most projects to make them pay off. Look at your failure and ask: "What was I not willing to risk—the time for proper education before jumping? The money to do the proper research? The effort to be persuasive?"

Just as an empty stall stays clean, an unexercised muscle doesn't get a cramp. But neither does it perform at its best. If you never take risks, you probably won't make a mistake, but neither will you enjoy the feeling of success.

Learn to think of risks as investments in your future. If all you have to show for your life so far is a clean stable or failure, then *act*.

We Learn to Follow God's Laws

God is a God of order, the Bible tells us, and that order often includes the causes and effects of our failures. If we are talking about financial failure, we may not have heeded God's admonition that the wise man cheerfully gives to the Lord the firstfruits of his labor and hears the cries of the poor. If we're talking about failure as a Christian businessperson standing against immorality, we may not have studied the Word of God and put on the whole armor against the day of evil in our lives.

We Become Aware of Our Strengths and Weaknesses

Although almost everyone does it from time to time, placing blame is seldom appropriate or fully accurate. We learn to quit blaming our family for "holding us back," our boss for "unclear directions," and our colleagues for not "warning us about what was ahead."

Researchers at the Center for Creative Leadership in Greensboro, North Carolina, recently asked seventy-six highly successful women in major corporations if they had ever failed on the job and taken a career misstep. Nearly three-quarters of the respondents reported at least one major setback. The most frequently mentioned failures were failure to sell one's ideas in the company and failure to carry through on ideas or assigned projects. Yet all these prominent, successful women ultimately succeeded because they pinpointed their *own* weaknesses and went to work on correcting those trouble spots.

We Learn to Overcome Shame

Since childhood, we have been programmed to consider, "What will they think of me?" If you act ashamed and defeated, people will treat you that way.

In 1963, fresh out of college, Lionel Aldridge began his life as pro football player with the Green Bay Packers and, as a part of that team, won three straight National Football League championships and the first two Super Bowls. His coach, Vince Lombardi, made a lasting impression on him as he talked of success not in terms of never falling down but in always rising up after a fall.

Due to a chemical imbalance, Lionel became schizophrenic. For years he refused the medication that would correct the problem because he was ashamed of the side effects: impotence, protruding tongue, stiffened arms and legs. For seven years he heard voices and could not function, losing his family, his job, and his friends. After he admitted his powerlessness to help himself, he sought help from medical treatment and was cured. No longer ashamed, he speaks to groups about his mental illness and recovery in an effort to dispel darkness over failure (*Parade Magazine*, March 1, 1987).

Companies fail, politicians fail, sports figures fail. Someone has said that failure is not contagious unless you act as though you are a carrier.

We Learn to Cope With Disappointment

There is nothing new about despair and depression. The psalmist David, the prophet Jonah, and the long-suffering Job were the most notably depressed writers in the Bible. Undoubtedly, at times the Apostle Paul, too, felt disappointed at being locked up in a prison cell rather than preaching on a street corner. He felt irritation at having to defend himself against false teachers and having to "prove" he was dedicated to the cause of the Gospel.

People throughout history have experienced a sense of depression and failure; Winston Churchill called it his "black dog." Neither was Abraham Lincoln a stranger to the feeling. Someone once summed up his road to the White

House like this: Failed in business in 1831. Defeated for legislature in 1832. Second failure in business in 1833. Suffered nervous breakdown in 1836. Defeated for speaker in 1838. Defeated for elector in 1840. Defeated for Congress in 1843. Defeated for Congress in 1848. Defeated for Senate in 1855. Defeated for vice-president in 1856. Defeated for Senate in 1858. Elected president in 1860.

Alexander Graham Bell was unable to sell his telephone to Western Union. Chester Carlson's idea of xerographic copying was rejected by several major corporations before it sparked the growth of Xerox Corporation. Computers originally left Tom Watson, head of IBM, very "nonplused" about their usefulness, and he reportedly estimated the world market for them to be about five buyers.

The *Wall Street Journal* reports that approximately 61,000 businesses in the United States failed in 1986. Others may be wrong in the way they react to our ideas and efforts, but today's failures may be tomorrow's biggest success stories. In the meantime, disappointment is part of the process. Disappointment is a part of the human condition that helps highlight times of satisfaction for a job well-done.

We Accept Our Inability to Control the World

Oh, sure, we all know that, in theory; it's only in practice that things get fuzzy. We can't control our health. We can't control our subordinates and make them want to do a good job. We can't control our bosses and make them give us the right decisions. We can't control industry flukes or the whims of the American consumer.

Yet, some businesspeople, through a series of successes that they have erroneously chalked up to their own efforts rather than to God's graciousness, come to feel invincible. It often takes the unpredictable to make us recognize God's control in our lives.

We Find New, More Worthy Goals

We may find new friends who have been through the same experiences and can encourage us. A change of activities can give us a totally new perspective.

Vincent van Gogh made that discovery with a change of goals. He came to his art in the last ten years of his life, having tried and failed at selling art, school teaching, and preaching, where the evangelical authorities dismissed him for his "excessive" zeal in helping Belgian coal miners. His brother supported him all his life because he sold only one picture for five francs. In the last three months of his life, van Gogh was still experimenting, striving toward his ideal; he painted twelve pictures in a new format, the double square. After lifelong bouts of mental illness and despair over his "failures," he took his own life. In 1987, his painting *Sunflowers* sold at a London auction for $39.9 million, more than three times the previous world-auction record. In 1988, his *Irises* set another world record—$53.9 million.

We Learn to Overcome Fear

God alone—not money or bosses or new ideas or our own expertise or hard work—controls our destiny. Perfect trust and love of Him casts out fear.

Failure is only failure when we fail to learn from our experiences.

For Further Reflection:

If you faint in the day of adversity, your strength is small.
Proverbs 24:10 RSV

In all toil there is profit, but mere talk tends only to want.
Proverbs 14:23 RSV

He that covereth his sins shall not prosper: but whoso confesseth and forsaketh them shall have mercy.
Proverbs 28:13

Trust in the Lord with all thine heart; and lean not unto thine own understanding. In all thy ways acknowledge him, and he shall direct thy paths.

Proverbs 3:5,6

And now I am about to go the way of all the earth, and you know in your hearts and souls, all of you, that not one thing has failed of all the good things which the Lord your God promised concerning you; all have come to pass for you, not one of them has failed.

Joshua 23:14 RSV

Be strong and of a good courage, fear not, nor be afraid of them: for the Lord thy God, he it is that doth go with thee; he will not fail thee, nor forsake thee.

Deuteronomy 31:6

3. Be Ye Kind to Your Customers

And as ye would that men should do to you, do ye also to them likewise.

Luke 6:31

And the King shall answer and say unto them, Verily I say unto you, Inasmuch as ye have done it unto one of the least of these my brethren, ye have done it unto me. . . . Then shall he answer them, saying, Verily I say unto you, Inasmuch as ye did it not to one of the least of these, ye did it not to me.

Matthew 25:40, 45

Like the proverbial average family that moves every five years, we got the itch to mow a new lawn. Finding the house of our dreams, we apply for a loan with Mortgage Company X, which guarantees in-house approval within thirty to forty-five days. "Will I need a CPA-prepared financial-worth statement since I'm self-employed?" I ask. "If so, I want to get it now, rather than slow up the process somewhere down the line."

"No problem," the loan officer answers. "If you keep your own books, your statement is good enough."

A few days later, the loan officer calls to say she has lost the VA eligibility certificate. Can we supply another? We do. A few days later she phones to say that they do, after all, need our CPA to prepare a statement. He does. We wait.

Finally approval comes. But two hours before closing, our realtor calls to say there will be no closing. Mortgage Company X does not intend to honor the "VA point" commitment they made at the time of application. Somehow the loan officer has never gotten around to putting it in writing for us. What's more, the loan officer in charge of our file has been fired.

After a conversation with our lawyer, who merely shakes his head, we drop by to see the person in charge at Mortgage Company X. A receptionist is holding down the fort. The head office has decided "to relieve from duty" all loan officers at that location, and others will be flying in shortly from headquarters to hear our complaints. A couple of days later, they permit us to quietly take our loan package to another institution. We run.

But that is just the beginning. After signing on the dotted line with Mortgage Company Y, we breathe a sigh of gratitude and pull out the home-furnishings catalogs. Custom window coverings come from Department Store A. The master bedroom woven-wood window covering is two inches too short and two inches too narrow. Would I mind if they just spray on a chemical treatment and "yank" it down? I say okay. They do. It doesn't work. They refund the money, and I'm only out a four-week delay.

I call Store B. Humming at the typewriter while the installer hangs the second wood covering, I dream of privacy in the bedroom. But the installer comes down the hall shaking his head. "You wanted a double-pull wood, Ma'am? I'm afraid the factory made a mistake. I'm going to have to send this back."

On Store B's second delivery, I'm afraid to look. "Ma'am," the installer says, "you're not going to believe this, but they made the same mistake. It's the same one we sent back." I get the correct window covering six weeks later.

Store C delivers a brass bed for my daughter's room. One hole for the frame is drilled higher than the other. "But it is a thirty-four-dollar special," the salesclerk reminds me on the phone. My husband drills a lower hole.

The master bedroom brass headboard, a more expensive variety, we don't dare trust to a delivery truck. The salesman will send it to package pickup while we pull the car around. He does and we do. In the bedroom light, after we've unloaded the headboard with (literally) gloved hands, we see the scratches—headboard to footboard. Yes, the salesman says on the phone, we can return it if we bring it back immediately. He "had a feeling" package pickup would be careless with it. "They do it all the time," he assures us. It is the only headboard of its kind in stock.

The following Saturday, Store D delivers the new washer; the old one, in its twelfth year, had washed its last load a week earlier. On the spin cycle, a smoky scent fills the house. The repairman says it can't possibly have a burned-out motor. It does.

After only two tries, Store E delivers the fireplace screen (without the screws) and a dinette. It seems they delivered both to the old billing address, rather than the one we had carefully printed on the contract under DELIVER TO. "Be glad to give you a refund on the fireplace screen if you want to bring it back," the clerk says. Is it worth the forty-five-minute trip across town? We find screws to fit at the corner hardware store and make do.

The garage-door opener we buy as an unassembled do-it-yourself kit. After installation the remote controls don't control. The store owner promises to have the manufacturer send new ones. They come ten days later, COD for sixty-two-dollars. After refusing the delivery, we phone the store again. Ownership has changed hands, and the new owner doesn't know about honoring the old guarantee. *Old* guarantee? Eleven days? My husband takes the opener off the garage door and returns it anyway. How can they refuse eyeball to eyeball? They do.

"If you'll come back tomorrow, when the repairman will be around to see that you haven't damaged the controls when you installed it, we'll see about a replacement," the new owner says. After the second forty-five-mile trip the following day, the repairman verifies that the remote controls never controlled. Our refund is uncheerfully given.

Have we been singled out for this persecution, we wonder. Is the rest of the world faring any better? Not even our daily newspaper will tell us; the paper's deliveryman argues that our street is nonexistent. Four days and two lengthy direction sessions later, we get a paper.

So much for the outside world. But can we make contact? I've always been one to get mail. The second week after our move, our mail dwindles to "Dear Occupant" circulars. A trip to our old address produces approximately an eight-inch stack of first class mail.

Yes, the postal supervisor says, they do still have the change-of-address notice on file. But they frequently have a sub on the route, and possibly nobody has told him to forward the mail. The supervisor will "take care of it personally." Four months and numerous phone calls later, we resort to removing the mailbox from the pole at our old address. They can't leave it there without a box, can they?

Anticipating such "disruptions of service," we had planned early phone installation: One month before M-Day, I call to have telephone service transferred and to ask for a cost estimate. A marketing specialist will have to call me back because my order is complicated. After hearing nothing for two weeks, I phone again. The representative apologizes for the delay and promises to give the order her personal attention. I ask if she can give me an assigned number; she does, insisting, of course, that the number can't be guaranteed until installation. I understand. Relying on the "ninety-six percent chance" that the number will work, I use the number in a national ad. The next day, the representative calls back to explain she made a mistake in assigning the number and figuring the charges.

Four weeks later, the installer phones me. He wants to know where I am. He's at the new residence to install the phone, and the house is empty. I tell him about the reschedule due to Mortgage Company X's shenanigans, giving him name, date, and hour of the rescheduling. He never got the word, he says. We reschedule for a week later.

I wait in a cold, empty house for the installer to arrive between 8:00 A.M. and 5:00 P.M. At 4:55, he shows up. The phone works, but the answering service will take another five days. Thank goodness for at least one inefficiency; they have failed to put the transfer tape on the old number. The outside world can still contact me.

Fifty-four days after my original order request, I have a working telephone. Rejoicing, I phone friends with the correct new number. But when I try to dial the downtown library, I can't. Have they done what I think they have? Yes. The operator verifies that they have installed a limited suburban line instead of the metro service I ordered.

Two days later, the bill arrives for one month's service. Since the phone has been working for only forty-six hours, I call to complain. "Not to worry," the representative tells me. She will adjust the bill and send a corrected copy.

Customer Relations calls to ask about "the manner in which my recent order has been handled." Is it worth fifteen minutes to tell her? I decide it is, giving her names and dates. "This is my job," she gushes, "to catch problems like this. I'm going to give this to my supervisor for his personal attention, and he'll get back to you."

A disruption-of-service notice arrives. I phone to say that I have never received a corrected bill. "We'll make a note not to disconnect, then," the representative says, "so don't worry." I do.

Two days later, the phone isn't working; my line is crossed with another number. They correct the problem twelve days later.

No one ever calls back from Customer Relations.

We all have our own horror stories, from an automobile with defective tires to chocolate-chip cupcakes with no chips from the supermarket bakery.

Has it always been so? Not necessarily. James Cash Penney, starting in 1902, built a multibillion-dollar business empire on the Golden Rule principle. In fact, for years his stores were called The Golden Rule Stores and operated on the principle of treating customers as the owner himself wanted to be treated.

Employees and their employers in the eighties certainly have been alerted to the decline of customer service and satisfaction. According to a study conducted for the American Society for Quality Control, 41 percent of corporate executives surveyed said that quality control will be the most critical business issue in the next three years. In fact, 57 percent said that improving product quality will be more important than increasing profits or reducing costs (*Small Business Report*, February 1987).

Disregard for the customer cannot be blamed on the lack of modern-day prophets. W. Edwards Deming and Joseph Juran, both sharing the reputation as the men who economically saved Japan after the war, have long preached their message of high quality in product development and manufacturing. To paraphrase Juran, American business operates on a policy of "take the money and run" rather than meeting the needs of customers over the lifetime of the product or service.

Many have put their finger directly on the hurt. But has American business listened?

When the average department hears that the CEO is coming for a visit, they spit and polish their operation until service shines. But do they not understand that God's visits come more regularly?

Look around your office. Would you sell the same products to the Lord, or would you advise Him to shop elsewhere for quality? Would your services be rendered more timely, carefully, or cheerfully if He were your customer? If you've done it (or not done it) to the least of these my brethren. . . .

For Further Reflection:

Let each of you look not only to his own interests, but also to the interests of others.

Philippians 2:4 RSV

4. Respect for Authority: Rendering Unto Caesar and Mrs. Jones

Remind them to be submissive to rulers and authorities, to be obedient, to be ready for any honest work.

Titus 3:1 RSV

Let every person be subject to the governing authorities. For there is no authority except from God, and those that exist have been instituted by God. Therefore he who resists the authorities resists what God has appointed, and those who resist will incur judgment. . . . For the same reason you also pay taxes, for the authorities are ministers of God, attending to this very thing. Pay all of them their dues, taxes to whom taxes are due, revenue to whom revenue is due, respect to whom respect is due, honor to whom honor is due.

Romans 13:1, 2, 6, 7 RSV

And Jesus answering said unto them, Render to Cae-
sar the things that are Caesar's, and to God the things
that are God's. And they marvelled at him.

Mark 12:17

"What you hide from the tax man can put you into beach-front property," a New York City Department of Finance ad promises. But what the ad is referring to as beachfront property is Rikers Island, the New Yorker's Alcatraz. Other ads try to humor the tax dodger. One such ad features a man in his home cheating on his income tax return. Then the scene fades to a penitentiary, where the same man sits behind bars with a file. The caption says, "You can file now, or you can file later."

Publicity campaigns to lure tax cheaters to pay up have become a last resort for many state and local governments suffering from those individual citizens who have decided to buck the taxing authority and write their own laws and loopholes.

Probably nowhere is our will to submit to authority in goverment tested more stridently than in the area of taxes.

How serious is the problem? A recent report by James J. O'Leary, Ph.D., economic consultant to the United States Trust Company of New York, estimates that in 1985, $431.7 billion in cash failed to get reported to the taxing authorities. In other words, Uncle Sam lost $43 billion in taxes due to cheaters. According to a recent *Working Woman* survey of 3,428 respondents, the figure on tax cheaters was one out of four citizens (*Working Woman*, April 1987).

According to another study by the market-research firm of Yankelovich, Skelly and White, Inc., one out of five citizens admits to some form of tax cheating; one in three thinks such behavior is expected and acceptable.

Do the ad campaigns work? Tom Riplette, Minnesota revenue commissioner quoted in a *Newsweek* interview, estimates that every dollar spent on enforcement publicity can yield between six dollars and seven dollars in recovered revenue.

But is it conscience that brings the cheaters around? No, government officials insist, it's simply the humiliation of public exposure. In other words, they care more about what men think of their cheating than about what God thinks.

A small-business owner recently confessed such a weakness—of which God alone had convicted him and for which he intended to make restitution. The business owner commented on the temptation he faced not to show all his income on the books and to add personal expenses to the corporate accounts. He came to the conclusion that these bookkeeping tactics were nothing less than stealing from the government and defying God-ordained authority.

That realization and turnaround comes almost exclusively with the understanding that our obedience to authority is at God's command.

But perhaps the authority even closer to many of us than the corporate tax books is the authority of our immediate supervisor on the job. The manager strides in and interrupts, "I need these reports ready by five tonight, and you need to cancel all further projects and out-of-town traveling until further notice."

"Who says?" a chorus of voices queries.

Sound familiar? People are still asking about the authority of those who give orders, just as the people in Jesus' day continually asked Him, "By what authority do You do these things?"

Human nature has always defied authority. It was that same proud attitude that cast Satan from heaven and resulted in the fall of man.

"High office is like a pyramid," says French philosopher d'Alembert. "Only two kinds of animals reach the summit, reptiles and eagles." We, as employees, prefer to be on an eagle's team and to defy, thwart, and bring down the reptiles.

But when Jesus said "Blessed are the meek," He did not

make the statement conditional on the personality of the one we must respect and defer to. Meekness is not weakness; it's willing submission.

Thoreau insisted, in his *Civil Disobedience*, "That government is best which governs least." Most businesspeople would agree, especially when Congress is about to pass legislation that directly affects their industry.

But the only biblical permission we have to disobey authority occurs where that authority directly defies God's laws. "We ought to obey God rather than men" (Acts 5:29). However, most of our disrespect and defiance of authority is not a result of being commanded to do something dishonest or immoral on the job; rather, our disrespect usually stems from self-interest: our dislike of an individual or an assigned task.

If employers could not count on respect for authority, our businesses would have little to distinguish them from cattle herds or amusement-park crowds. Respect for authority is an act and attitude of humility, self-denial, care of the common good of our business and society, and faith in God's providence. Submission to authority is victory over our uncivilized nature.

For Further Reflection:

For rebellion is as the sin of witchcraft, and stubbornness is as iniquity and idolatry. . . .

1 Samuel 15:23

Obey them that have the rule over you, and submit yourselves: for they watch for your souls, as they that must give account, that they may do it with joy, and not with grief: for that is unprofitable for you.

Hebrews 13:17

You slaves must always obey your earthly masters, not only trying to please them when they are watching you but all the time; obey them willingly because of your love for the Lord and because you want to please him. Work hard and cheerfully at all you do, just as though you were working for the Lord and not merely for your masters, remembering that it is the Lord Christ who is going to pay you, giving you your full portion of all he owns. He is the one you are really working for.

Colossians 3:22–24 TLB

5. How God Reads the Bottom Line

The Lord demands fairness in every business deal. He established this principle. It is a horrible thing for a king to do evil. His right to rule depends upon his fairness.

Proverbs 16:11, 12 TLB

The integrity of the upright shall guide them: but the perverseness of transgressors shall destroy them.

Proverbs 11:3

Every way of a man is right in his own eyes: but the Lord pondereth the hearts.

Proverbs 21:2

Better is a little with righteousness than great revenues without right.

Proverbs 16:8

We have a new corporate function floating around now: ethics consultant. The Boesky-Levine insider trading scandal has flashed a spotlight on Wall Street and made executives all over the country take note of questions of right and wrong again. Specifically, former Securities and Exchange Commission Chairman John Shad gave Harvard Business School $20 million to establish a program in ethics.

That's good, because for the past few years, we've been throwing around the term *situation ethics* as if there were such a thing. By definition, ethics are an absolute standard of right and wrong—morality versus immorality. If it's situational, it's not ethics.

We have problems determining what is and what is not a quality product or service. Every year we see the concerned media publish lists of unsafe toys to avoid as Christmas gifts. In early 1987, Eastern Airlines agreed to pay the largest civil penalty ever collected by the government—$9.5 million—for violation of 53 federal safety regulations. The violations included maintenance irregularities, improperly deferred repairs, and planes flown without the minimum equipment.

We have problems determining appropriate wages for employees, yet Luke 10:7 and James 5:4 tell us that a laborer is worthy of adequate, honest wages.

We keep lawyers busy handling cases where our word is not our bond. We keep ourselves covered in our own paperwork because no one trusts oral directions, directives, or confirmations.

We have problems with people taking advantage of the little guy. Someone has said that there is much more thievery going on in front of the counter than behind it. Big companies often take advantage of their small suppliers by asking for bigger and bigger volume discounts, threatening to take their business elsewhere. For suppliers and vendors who depend on a few large customers, this tactic almost always works. The alternative is simply to close the front door and turn out the light.

We have problems with people claiming credit for work they didn't do and facts they don't have. According to a 1985 congressional investigation, as many as 500,000 Americans hold fraudulent degrees (*Wall Street Journal*, April 2, 1987).

And the scientific community is not immune from equally flagrant deceptions. A recent publication titled "False Prophets," by Alexander Kohn of Tel Aviv Medical School, explores the reasons behind such frauds among scientists. A well-publicized fraud at Harvard Medical School involved the testing of heart drugs on dogs. Other such examples abound. In a publish-or-perish environment, evidently many have chosen to publish and pray no one verifies.

We have problems with bribes and payoffs. The National Collegiate Athletic Association repeatedly blows the whistle on coaches and administrators and boards of directors who tuck improper payments into the hands of amateur players for clothes, cars, and carousing. School officials who try to squelch the practices often lose their jobs.

We have problems with corporate stealing. Video and audio companies offering free previews of their materials frequently catch potential customers illegally copying their tapes. And some thieves are so blatant as to photograph their competitors' product designs at trade shows and then go back to their own drawing board to duplicate the designs.

Electronic eavesdroppers repeatedly underbid their competition by very slim margins and always seem to be one step ahead on marketing strategies and advertising campaigns. In fact, this problem is so prevalent that businesses are advised to keep the main telephone frame room secured and to ask all service technicians for identification.

Further, they are advised not to place telephones, tape recorders, or any electronic devices in rooms where confidential discussions are conducted. If those precautions don't curtail the stealing, they routinely have "debugging sweeps," including radio frequency analysis and physical searches performed by a security firm.

So what can be done about these "situation ethics" problems?

Employee training has been touted as the answer to a

multitude of problems in the workplace, and the chaos created by a floating ethical standard has been no exception. Executives are calling in consultants and house trainers to give crash courses on right and wrong.

But I'm of the opinion that by the time the individual gets to the marketplace, his or her ethical mind-set is fairly well coded. Little—short of conversion and God's conviction—can change that inner code from "The end justifies the means" to "The methods forecast the end."

And that change of conscience as an individual employee may cost your job. Such was the case with William B. Walton, one of the cofounders of the Holiday Inn chain. In his recent book *The New Bottom Line*, he says he resigned because the company's current policies departed from the founders' evangelical religious principles.

Then again, playing the part of the corporate conscience as a whistle-blower can be even more dangerous. Such was the case of Marie Ragghaianti, who as the head of the Tennessee Board of Pardons and Paroles in 1977 discovered that the administration was engaged in a conspiracy to sell early prison releases to inmates and their families. At first, her choice seemed to be between looking the other way or resigning. She chose neither; she went to the FBI.

Likewise, in the early 1970s, a New York City police officer named Frank Serpico uncovered graft in his own police force. When his efforts to clean up the corruption from within failed, he opted for the front page of the *New York Times*. He was shot.

Marie Ragghaianti, writing of her experiences and those of others who have stood up for their convictions, insists that their real motives were triumphs of decisions made long before the time and place when they would be tested. They had decided long ago to be true to their personal convictions, regardless of what others thought and regardless of the physical consequences (*Parade Magazine*, March 22, 1987).

If you haven't come to a similar decision or test, consider

what's at stake when you violate God's clear-cut principles of conducting business or simply surviving in the marketplace. In the final pay period, whose payroll do you want to be on?

For Further Reflection:

A man's conscience is the Lord's searchlight exposing his hidden motives. If a king is kind, honest and fair, his kingdom stands secure.

Proverbs 20:27, 28 TLB

We have renounced disgraceful, underhanded ways; we refuse to practice cunning or to tamper with God's word, but by the open statement of the truth we would commend ourselves to every man's conscience in the sight of God.

2 Corinthians 4:2 RSV

For we aim at what is honorable not only in the Lord's sight but also in the sight of men.

2 Corinthians 8:21 RSV

Help me to refuse the low and vulgar things; help me to abhor all crooked deals of every kind, to have no part in them.

Psalms 101:3 TLB

The Lord despises every kind of cheating. The character of even a child can be known by the way he acts—whether what he does is pure and right.

Proverbs 20:10, 11 TLB

For the ways of man are before the eyes of the Lord, and he pondereth all his goings.

Proverbs 5:21

Blessed are they who observe justice, who do righteousness at all times!

Psalms 106:3 RSV

6. Stealing Your Shirt and Computer Database

Thou shalt not steal.

Exodus 20:15

Dishonest gain will never last, so why take the risk?

Proverbs 21:6 TLB

Retail stores call it *inventory shrinkage;* supermarkets refer to it as *spoilage.* If we throw away the euphemisms, we're talking about theft. But the thief isn't solely the consumer. A U.S. Department of Commerce study reveals that theft on the job costs U.S. businesses $40 billion annually. In 1986, the U.S. Chamber of Commerce reported that 75 percent of all employees steal at least once from their employer; 40 percent have stolen more often.

According to Dr. Paul Mok, chairman of Training Associates, a company that conducts seminars on business ethics, more than one hundred banks and savings and loan institutions failed in 1985 due to criminal acts of their senior management (*Houston Chronicle,* May 19, 1986).

The FBI estimates that $300 million in annual bank losses occur through computer embezzlement.

Ron Zemke, editor of *Training Magazine* (May 1986), cites several studies that also pinpoint the thief as employee. A recent study of retail businesses done by Arthur Young, the international accounting and consulting firm, revealed that merchants assigned 43 percent of their losses from theft to employees and only 30 percent to shoplifters. And according to Dennis Joy, director of security testing for London House, approximately 80 percent of all employee theft goes undetected!

Nevertheless, employees themselves admit their guilt. Stanton Corporation, a North Carolina firm specializing in theft prevention in the workplace, reports that in a survey of 7,000 retail job applicants, 30 percent admitted to stealing at least $10 worth of merchandise from a former employer. The average "take" of these employees was $33.97.

Then we must consider stealing that may not directly involve hard cash. Some people make copies of all their company's software and sell it on the side. They don't consider this stealing because they insist their own companies are unharmed.

Preliminary results of a government-wide survey revealed that between 29 percent and 50 percent of all long-distance calls made by federal employees at five agencies were personal calls having nothing to do with their job assignments.

And the theft of trade secrets is a temptation in corporations of all sizes.

Is employee theft a relatively new concern? Well, not new, exactly, but it's certainly on the increase. Twenty years ago, the J.C. Penney company did not even prosecute employee theft; today the company keeps the *shrinkage* problem in front of its employees at all times. Managers, as well as part-time clerks, have to submit to package inspections as they leave the premises.

To combat this human propensity for stealing, employers primarily rely on two methods: lie detector tests—although there are currently nineteen states that prohibit such testing for preemployment screening—and paper and pencil "integrity" tests.

Just how far our society has come on business ethics and stealing in particular was brought home to me recently in a comment from my high-school-age son, who was asked to take one of these "integrity" tests before part-time employment at a local supermarket. At dinner he confided to his father and me: "I'm kind of worried about that test they had me take today. They had questions like: 'Have you ever taken drugs?' 'Do you drink alcohol?' 'Have you ever cheated in school?' 'Have you ever stolen money from your parents?' 'Have you ever stolen anything from a schoolmate or an employer?' When I started answering no to all those, I started worrying that they'd think I was lying because I sounded too good to be true."

Although his concern was unfounded and he did get the job, I had to reflect on the state of society when teenagers feel uneasy about being too honest!

We see a breakdown in morality and open acceptance of crooked practices everywhere, whether it's stealing a job by falsifying a résumé and buying a diploma for $500 or making personal copies on the company copier. I see children with no models, no standards, no discipline, and no respect for an authority who tells them stealing is wrong.

Although employers are currently coming to grips with the problem by offering training in the form of videos and seminar discussions to inform employees of the seriousness of being caught, many still ponder the question: "Can you train an employee to be honest?"

Perhaps employees can be informed about policies and penalties, but motivation for honesty comes only from inner conviction. Whatever the temptation—long-distance phone calls, a box of chocolate éclairs, padded expense accounts, or unauthorized computer access to the Dow Jones News Retrieval Service—"Thou shalt not steal" covers them all.

For Further Reflection:

The partner of a thief hates his own life; he hears the curse, but discloses nothing.

Proverbs 29:24 RSV

Ill-gotten gain brings no lasting happiness; right living does.

Proverbs 10:2 TLB

A little, gained honestly, is better than great wealth gotten by dishonest means.

Proverbs 16:8 TLB

Dishonest money brings grief to all the family, but hating bribes brings happiness.

Proverbs 15:27 TLB

Better to be poor and honest than rich and a cheater.

Proverbs 28:6 TLB

7. The Author of Creativity

For in him we live, and move, and have our being; as certain also of your own poets have said, For we are also his offspring.

Acts 17:28

"Everything that can be invented has been invented." That comment was made by Charles Duell, Director of the United States Patent Office—in 1899.

Who would have thought that by the 1990s we'd have mud wrestling, no-fault divorce, plea bargaining for criminals, music by computers, T-shirts with messages, soyburgers, men's perfume, garage-door openers, diet pills, surrogate mothers, personal shopper services, and note brokers?

A young clerk got an idea to open a store that would sell only nickel and dime items. In his own mind, he had figured all the angles. He would run the store, and his boss could supply the money for the inventory and operating capital.

No deal, the boss responded on hearing the idea; finding that many items to sell for a nickel or dime would be impossible. But F. W. Woolworth certainly made a go of it on his own.

Most of us, however, are afraid to roll with our ideas. My brother called yesterday, wanting my reaction to a new idea for his own business. After explaining his creative concept and assuring me that there was nothing like it in the Dallas–Fort Worth area, he asked if I'd heard of such a business in my part of the country. When I assured him I hadn't, the tone in his voice was one of disappointment rather than happiness. His reasoning? If no one else had thought of this business concept, the idea was probably unsound.

Why do we doubt our own perception and creativity? It's highly likely that none of us, my brother included, has thought enough about what being made in God's own image means.

Certainly, the most striking example of creativity is described in Genesis. From nothing, God created something. Because the Bible tells us that we live, move, and exist by His power, we, too, can participate in divine creativity if we permit God to use us in this way. Certainly the young prophet Daniel came up with a creative way to meet the king of Babylon's objective that his captives be physically fit. Likewise, when two women both claiming to be the mother of the same child came to King Solomon, he came up with a creative way of determining the real mother.

God is equally ready to help His present-day followers with creative ideas and solutions.

Using our innate creative natures is not a new focus in modern-day business. Way back in 1937, General Electric began a creative engineering program for employees who proved promising within their first two months of employment. And in 1954, the Creative Education Foundation of Buffalo, New York, was founded to teach creativity to corporations. Since that time, creativity training has become almost a fad, and even the largest companies—including

Exxon, IBM, General Motors, Colgate-Palmolive, and Shell Oil—have paid consultants up to $2,000 a day to teach their employees how to think creatively.

Even though experts can't agree on a definition of creativity, they all conclude that we can focus and use our creativity by practicing a few techniques.

Brainstorming

A group of individuals generates as many ideas as they can to solve a problem. Someone records all the ideas without permitting evaluation or criticism at this stage. Then participants cluster and categorize the ideas, evaluate their potential, and recommend the best solution for the problem.

Synectics

The two men who set forth this method of creative thinking (George Price and W. J. J. Gordon) are making the strange familiar. Let me oversimplify this method: A problem is analyzed and then reinterpreted in terms of an analogy. A new viewpoint is defined and superimposed over the original problem to frame a new way of looking at the problem and its solution. For example: If sunlight interacts with chlorophyll to make plants green, what would it take to react with X substance to make this product turn a different color?

Brainwriting

This technique, developed by Bernd Rohrback, is relatively simple. After a problem or situation is presented, individuals are given a blank piece of paper and are asked to write four or five solutions, suggestions, or merely thoughts about the problem or situation. They then exchange the paper with someone else and continue the process by writing the thoughts generated in them from reading the thoughts of the previous person.

Lists

Individuals are given a checklist of questions or topic prompts. The items on the checklist act as cues to spur the individuals into new ways of considering a problem. For example: If we are thinking of a new way to print a newsletter, we might have come up with new ideas for layout, form, design, and content by moving through a checklist that asks certain questions. Can it be made smaller or larger? Can it be a different color? Can it be made with a different piece of equipment? Can it serve more than one purpose? Should it be done quicker? Should it be done slower? Could it be done cheaper? Could it be done more expensively?

Lateral Thinking

Lateral thinking encourages people to move out of the mode of logical reasoning. Instead, individuals try to rearrange the information they have about a situation and discard old assumptions about what can and can't be done. Primarily, they challenge all "givens" to a situation and develop new ways of looking at a problem.

For example, the problem or situation might be presented: "We cannot keep large sums of money on the premises. How can we find a dependable van driver to deliver our money to the bank on schedule four times a day?" Participants begin to challenge that thinking and those logical assumptions: Why can't we keep large sums of money on the premises? Why drive the money to a bank? Could we use a plane rather than a van? Why four times a day? Maybe we should not deal in cash at all?

Force-Fitting

This creative-thinking technique encourages individuals to take two seemingly unrelated ideas, even outrageous ideas, and jam them together into one solution—modifying, squeezing, twisting, reducing, or enlarging the ideas to see if they can possibly be made into a reasonable solution or an altogether new option. For example: How could you make writing stationery smell nice? How could you talk on the phone while driving? We know the results of those force-fitting ideas, but here's another one still under development: How can you eat all the high-caloric foods you desire and still look slim and be healthy?

How do these creative-thinking techniques sound to you? Before you answer that, let me mention how personality and environment fit into the picture.

Creativity seems to flourish in environments where there is both freedom to think and guided control toward a purpose. There have to be sufficient resources, high trust, acceptance of failure, the opportunity to try again for success, and open communication with others. People who flourish in these environments are those who are self-motivated to be the best they can be and do the best they can do, who have good analytical skills, and who aren't afraid to make mistakes.

Consider the reverse. Creativity is usually stifled in an environment where things are tightly controlled, where no one has the money or the time to think, where people are not rewarded for doing their best. People who are inflexible, who lack motivation, and who have little expertise or experience stifle their own creative impulses.

Therefore, as Christian businesspeople wanting to use the creativity God gave us, we should make sure our offices, churches, and homes foster creative thinking.

The Author of creativity is on our side. Creative thinking is often simply a matter of a pair of fresh eyes.

For Further Reflection:

Therefore if any man be in Christ, he is a new creature: old things are passed away; behold, all things are become new.

2 Corinthians 5:17

First Thing Monday Morning

In the beginning God created the heavens and the earth.

Genesis 1:1 RSV

Thou art worthy, O Lord, to receive glory and honour and power: for thou hast created all things, and for thy pleasure they are and were created.

Revelation 4:11

All things were made by him; and without him was not any thing made that was made.

John 1:3

Create in me a clear heart, O God; and renew a right spirit within me.

Psalms 51:10

8. The Two-Career Family: Part 1

Who can find a virtuous woman? for her price is far above rubies. The heart of her husband doth safely trust in her, so that he shall have no need of spoil. She will do him good and not evil all the days of her life. She seeketh wool, and flax, and worketh willingly with her hands. She is like the merchants' ships; she bringeth her food from afar. She riseth also while it is yet night, and giveth meat to her household, and a portion to her maidens. She considereth a field, and buyeth it: with the fruit of her hands she planteth a vineyard. She girdeth her loins with strength, and strengtheneth her arms. She perceiveth that her merchandise is good: her candle goeth not out by night. She layeth her hands to the spindle, and her hands hold the distaff. She stretcheth out her hand to the poor; yea, she reacheth forth her hands to the needy. She is not afraid of the snow for her household: for all her household are clothed with scarlet. She maketh herself coverings of tapestry; her clothing is silk and purple. Her husband is known in the gates, when he sitteth among the elders of the land. She maketh fine linen, and selleth it; and delivereth girdles unto the merchant. Strength and honour are her clothing; and she shall rejoice in time to come. She openeth her mouth with wisdom; and in her tongue is the law of kindness. She looketh well to the ways of her household, and eateth not the bread of idleness. Her children arise up, and call her blessed; her husband also, and he praiseth her. Many daughters have done virtuously, but thou excellest them all. Favour is deceitful, and beauty is vain: but a woman that feareth the Lord, she shall be praised. Give her of the fruit of her hands; and let her own works praise her in the gates.

Proverbs 31:10–31

Probably no other issue affecting the family has had so much press coverage in the last twenty years as women joining the work force in mass. In fact, women now comprise just under 45 percent of the total United States work force. The 1980 census was the first to report that slightly over half (52 percent) of all women are now employed outside the home. And a whopping 67 percent of all women between the ages of 18 and 34 (in other words, mothers) hold a job outside the home.

We've read conflicting reports from clergy and psychologists, schoolteachers, and counselors about the effects of that transition on our society. While some cite studies to show that children in homes where both parents work are brighter, more secure, more responsible, and more cooperative, other spokespersons lay almost all the evils of America at the doorstep of working women.

Whether a woman is the sole means of support for herself and her children due to a disabled, absent, or unwilling-to-work husband, or whether a woman works because she and her family consider it part of God's plan for their lives, the fact remains: The majority of women have taken on an additional role, as well as the traditional role.

In Proverbs, we find a virtuous woman who has assumed both roles. She tends well to the ways of her household and husband, and she buys and sells fields and merchandise. Evidently she is successful in both roles to the extent that she is praised for her efforts. This is definitely not the picture of a harried household, unhappy, maladjusted children, and a hostile husband. So how does she do it?

Dara (name changed to protect the guilty) was panicky as she waved me out of her house after I brought over a package left with me by UPS. Her husband was bringing home dinner guests, and the sight wasn't encouraging. She had rattles and stuffed animals from wall to wall, patterns of bunny-rabbit costumes cut from old newspapers slung over the dining room table, piles of unfolded laundry on the sofa, strings all over the carpet, stacks of dishes from the sink to the refrigerator, empty milk cartons and cereal boxes on the breakfast-nook windowsill, and three red negligees hanging over the Japanese partition into the hallway (she sold lingerie on the side).

No, Dara did not consider herself a working woman. She spent her day volunteering for church and school projects, directing her community drama club (the bunny costumes), playing tennis, and campaigning for a city-council representative.

Disorganization and priority pileups happen to the best. Stay-at-home wives and mothers don't necessarily have clean, organized homes and well-adjusted, happy children and husbands, anymore than their counterparts in the business world. And they don't necessarily stay at home all day.

Therefore, women who assume both the traditional and the additional roles should stop flagellating themselves because they can't get it all done and find ways to improve the quality of life for all the family.

I call it hands-on experience with inventory control, project management, delegation and supervision, accountability, and quality control.

Inventory Control

My daughter's favorite trick used to be to leave a note on the dinner table saying, "I need panty hose for school in the morning" or "I'm supposed to have a girl's gift to exchange at gym class at 2:25 today." With a supermarket and drugstore on every corner, children (and sometimes adults) do not realize the inefficiency of running out of things. Don't be caught up in operating an errand-and-delivery service at your house. Keep adequate stock of the necessities, whether it's cans of tomato juice or shoelaces. (I didn't say buying a birthday gift before you know who the birthday girl is, is easy—just efficient!)

Project Management

We do it for vacations; we can do it for the smaller projects. Before we leave on a trip, don't we usually consider what has to be done, when, with what, and by whom?

Apply the same principles to other projects, whether it's attending a two-day meeting at your church or shopping for school clothes. Plan.

Delegation and Supervision

Working mothers soon learn the difference between assigning chores and delegation. Assigning children chores is: "Johnny, I want you to carry out the trash this minute. Don't forget the trash can in the hall bathroom. And be sure to tie up the bag with those stronger twist ties." Delegating is: "Johnny, your responsibility is to put out all the trash each week. The garbage collectors come before noon on Mondays and Thursdays." It's up to Johnny to decide when and how it's done—just as long as the desired results are achieved. And that brings us to the next point.

Accountability

Family members who are responsible for various family projects learn from them. They not only learn to work, they learn to plan, to make decisions, to budget their time, to be successful. Through supervision with resulting rewards and penalties, they learn what it feels like to do a complete project well, to be trusted, to be self-sufficient, to accept directions, to be dependable, to contribute to the common good of the family. In short, they learn to be successful adults.

Quality Control

Mothers most likely are the ones to check on family atmosphere and goals with, "Hey, are we having fun yet?" In an atmosphere where husband and wife are supposed to be mutually submissive and loving to each other and where children are submissive to their parents, there should be quality life as God defined it for the home. If that is not the case, do some serious questioning.

- Who feels left out?
- Who needs more time from whom?
- Can we watch TV less?
- What chores can we leave undone with nobody caring?
- Who is involved in too many outside activities at the expense of the family?
- When was the last time we spent a long weekend together?
- When was the last time we as a family participated in an extended worship experience such as a retreat?
- When was the last time we played a game or took in a family movie?
- Is one member of the family doing most of the sacrificing and work to keep things running smoothly?
- Is one member of the family forcing everyone else to sacrifice to keep his or her own schedule and goals on target?

- What are the family's financial goals, educational goals, and spiritual goals for the next five years? What do *we all* have to do to reach them?

Keeping the quality of homelife high is no easier than it is in the workplace, but the rewards are worth far more.

Rarely do working wives and mothers have to chastise themselves about "eating the bread of idleness." Instead, we all need to focus on organizing, planning, sharing, and giving attention to quality life. Those will mean the difference between a harried home and a haven.

For Further Reflection:

Whatsoever thy hand findeth to do, do it with thy might; for there is no work, nor device, nor knowledge, nor wisdom, in the grave, whither thou goest.

Ecclesiastes 9:10

9. The Two-Career Family: Part 2

Submitting yourselves one to another in the fear of God. Wives, submit yourselves unto your own husbands, as unto the Lord. For the husband is the head of the wife, even as Christ is the head of the church: and he is the saviour of the body. Therefore as the church is subject unto Christ, so let the wives be to their own husbands in every thing. Husbands, love your wives, even as Christ also loved the church, and gave himself for it. . . . So ought men to love their wives as their own bodies. He that loveth his wife loveth himself.

Ephesians 5:21–25, 28

Having just concluded a seminar at 5:00 P.M., I dashed toward the phones in the lobby to call home before heading out in the traffic. At the two busy phones ahead of me were two male executives in standard pinstriped suits and ties. They were involved, I was sure, in some last-minute corporate deal making. As I stood waiting my turn, I couldn't help but overhear both conversations.

The monologue to my left went something like this: "I'm still tied up in a meeting, and I'm not going to be home for dinner. Would you please get my suit out of the cleaners before they close? . . . Yeah, I'll meet you there. And one more thing, bring the checkbook. . . . "

I glanced to my right to see if the conversation there was winding down. Not much chance. The guy was bent over, scribbling something on a scrap of paper. A new offer in the negotiations? Then I heard, "Yeah, okay, I got it. Two boxes of orange Jell-O. . . ."

Needless to say, I smiled approvingly. More and more men are rethinking their roles as husband and father and doing more than simply bringing home the bacon. Their jobs today may involve Jell-O, birthday presents, and prescription medicine.

The idea of mutual submission and love and support between husbands and wives is not new. I saw my grandfather, a salt miner, cattleman, and vegetable farmer, wash the family dishes more than I saw my grandmother do it. He also helped can vegetables, hang out the laundry, and buy the groceries. She, in turn, worked in a factory for years and then, as retirement age approached, she took an "easier" job as a department-store salesclerk. In other words, before they died last year in their eighties, those two longtime believers learned what love, mutual submission, and mutual support were.

Although pollsters now tell us that most husbands give lip service to the idea that men should participate around the house in family responsibilities, for some, the intention or belief has not become reality. What do I mean by *participate?* How can husbands really tune in to their families' needs?

Emotional Support

Some men still think of their own on-the-job pressures and schedule hassles as having top priority. When a child complains about having difficulty with his math teacher, instead of listening and understanding, the father's response is: "Well, son, you're just going to have to deal with that. Out in the real world, like I face every day. . . ."

When a wife attempts to share a problem at work, rather than listening or offering practical advice, her husband cuts his eyes back to the newspaper with: "Well, just quit, then. You don't have to work." That kind of comment tells the wife her problems are minimal and petty compared to his, that she is bringing it all upon herself by taking on something she can't handle.

Verbal Encouragement

A selfish husband usually belittles a wife's bonus as "better than nothing," downplays the promotion as "to be expected," and insists the two-day training sessions away from home are an interruption and imposition on his personal schedule. A participating husband shares his wife's excitement over a promotion, a chance at more education, a bonus, an opportunity to travel and broaden her experiences, or a position on a worthwhile committee.

Sharing Excitement and Defeats

He lets her know when he's about to close a big deal or when he blew the presentation and didn't pull it off as planned. He calls home while he's attending a convention in Miami to tell her about the best restaurant meal he's ever eaten, and brings her a small gift to say she was missed. He sums up the day's meetings knowing she is an intelligent person who appreciates his expertise.

A selfish husband brushes off questions from a concerned wife with, "You wouldn't understand" or "I don't have time to go into it with you."

When I occasionally ask an acquaintance or friend what her husband does for a living, I'm always amazed how many times I get answers such as, "He works for XYZ Company. I don't know exactly what he does there. Something to do with oil." I didn't say I was amazed at the *wife's* unconcern or ignorance; often the lack of communication can be traced to a husband who doesn't care about participating in the family enough to include his wife in his day-to-day life. Wives have been warned to expect this kind of silent treatment if their husbands work for the CIA or the underworld, but not with normal jobs.

Help With the Mental and Menial Tasks

Although I appreciated the supportive executive husband who was stopping by the store for two boxes of Jell-O, somebody had to remember the promise to take the Jell-O salad to the church dinner and call him with a reminder. Sometimes, for the working mother, the problem's not the effort of actually wrapping the birthday presents; it's the responsibility of deciding how much you can afford to spend, finding out what the child wants or needs, and telephone shopping for the best price. Going by the store to pick up the gift may be the least of the effort.

A nonparticipating husband does only what he's asked. He vacuums up the mulch spilled on the carpet, and he takes out the garbage. A participating husband, on the other hand, assumes overall responsibility for some things—the remembering as well as the actual doing. He helps to see that the house is clean before the in-laws come, or he remembers to take the child to get his or her immunizations before school starts.

Quality Control

Finally, a participating husband checks the results of his emotional support, his praise and encouragement, their sharing of mutual concerns and responsibilities. Are all family members happy? Are all communicating? Are all spending quality time together as a family? Is the family meeting financial, emotional, and spiritual goals? If not, why not?

It may be up to the participating, mutually submissive husband to let the family, especially his wife, know when they're not getting a good return on their investment. "Hey, hon, why are you spending so much time in the kitchen on the weekends? Why don't we have sandwiches or Chinese take-out vegetables more often? I'd rather have you sitting in here with the kids and me."

To love a wife and family as Christ loved the Church often requires more investment than bringing home two boxes of orange Jell-O. But the emotional and spiritual return outperforms all other investments.

For Further Reflection:

But if any provide not for his own, and specially for those of his own house, he hath denied the faith, and is worse than an infidel.

1 Timothy 5:8

10. Lying and Living With the Boss

Lying lips are abomination to the Lord: but they that deal truly are his delight.

Proverbs 12:22

The getting of treasures by a lying tongue is a vanity tossed to and fro of them that seek death.

Proverbs 21:6

The majority of us don't butt our heads against big lies involving nonexistent corporate takeover plans or trade secrets. Rather, we deal with small-scale lies that make everyone wary.

An Excuse Booth provides patrons of about eighty bars across the United States with just what they'll need to get back into the office without questions. This Excuse Booth is a TV sound studio in a phone booth. For fifty cents it will play background noises of your choosing while you offer your lie to the person on the other end of the line.

If you want to use flight cancellations and delays as an excuse, you can select airport announcements and jet takeoff and landing noises. If you want to complain about the weather, you can select the rainstorm effect. If it's a retirement gala you've told someone you're attending, the background tape creates an instant party, complete with laughter, conversation, and clinking glasses.

Do people really use these booths? *Newsweek* (April 28, 1986) reports that one California booth owner needed a repair crew after the first day of operation: The coin slot became clogged with quarters.

But, you may be thinking, lying is a way of life only for office deadbeats, for husbands and wives cheating on their spouses, or for drunks and drug addicts holing up in these bars with their Excuse Booths.

Lying, however, has become a way of office life for many pinstriped Christians as well.

You have a problem: You're late for the meeting—again. The truth is that you and a friend got to talking golf over Chinese food and simply didn't get back to the office on time. The solution: Have your secretary tell your client that you were called out suddenly for an emergency. The result: Your client will rarely believe it, but he will nod and smile begrudgingly, remembering the last time he used the same line.

You have a phone call from someone you'd rather not talk to. The solution is delivered through your secretary: "He's in conference right now." "She's in a meeting." "She's on the other line." The result: Loss of productivity for both your office and the caller because both will have to call and respond several more times before the message is clear. The truth is easier. Conveyed through you or your secretary, it might be: "I'm not interested in the product (service) at this time," or "I'm very involved on a project this afternoon. May I call you back tomorrow?" Or "I don't have the information you need, but I suggest you call Ellen Brown."

Business owners lie to their suppliers and customers about delivery dates, prices, discounts, and terms.

Editors and publishers lie in their advertisements to store owners about how many copies of a book they print.

Accountants lie to their creditors with the cliché we all love to hate, "Your check is in the mail."

Salespeople, falling short of slanderous comments, misrepresent and lie about their competitors' products and services.

Bookkeepers lie to auditors with their alterations and their explanations about their reasoning. The SEC regulations require every public company "to make and keep books, records, and accounts, which, in reasonable detail, accurately and fairly reflect the transactions and dispositions of the assets of the issue." Playing games with a petty-cash voucher or an employee time card is an illegal lie. And what's more, computers that disguise altered records make the temptation to lie even stronger.

Allen I. Young, general counsel at Price Waterhouse, points out in *Price Waterhouse Review* (1986) the fraud and dangers in what is termed *cute accounting* or *loopholing*. If caught, the people who lie in these ways can always point out a chapter and verse in accounting literature that, they claim, led them to such erroneous thinking. Their rationalizations rarely wash with the IRS because they know they are following only the letter of the law rather than the substance.

It's not that most of us aren't aware of God's attitude about all lying but that, unlike the psalmist, we haven't made this verse our prayer: "Remove from me the way of lying: and grant me thy law graciously" (Psalms 119:29).

To term all such situations as lying sounds a little harsh because we generally sort falsehoods into several categories: whoppers, black lies, white lies, and almost-truths. I'm not sure God does.

For Further Reflection:

A false witness shall not be unpunished, and he that speaketh lies shall not escape.

Proverbs 19:5

Lying and Living With the Boss

What is desired in a man is loyalty, and a poor man is better than a liar.

Proverbs 19:22 RSV

Lies will get any man into trouble, but honesty is its own defense. Telling the truth gives a man great satisfaction, and hard work returns many blessings to him.

Proverbs 12:13, 14 TLB

Wherefore putting away lying, speak every man truth with his neighbour: for we are members one of another.

Ephesians 4:25

11. Delegation and Letting Della Do It

The next day Moses sat as usual to hear the people's complaints against each other, from morning to evening.

When Moses' father-in-law saw how much time this was taking, he said, "Why are you trying to do all this alone, with people standing here all day long to get your help? . . . Moses, this job is too heavy a burden for you to try to handle all by yourself.

"Now listen, and let me give you a word of advice, and God will bless you. . . . Find some capable, godly, honest men who hate bribes, and appoint them as judges. . . . Let these men be responsible to serve the people with justice at all times. Anything that is too important or complicated can be brought to you. But the smaller matters they can take care of themselves. That way it will be easier for you because you will share the burden with them. If you follow this advice, and if the Lord agrees, you will

*be able to endure the pressures, and there will be
peace and harmony in the camp."*

Exodus 18:14, 18, 19, 21, 22, 23 TLB

Are you irreplaceable?

Do you skip vacations or take your time off only a couple of days at a time?

Do you try to keep up with everybody's activities and whereabouts, rather than simply keeping up with their accomplishments?

Are you working longer hours than you'd like to?

Are your people having to transfer around you to move up in the company?

Do you always seem to have somebody waiting to talk to you about something before they can go further with their work?

Do you manage to phone into the office every day while you're off during an illness or while attending a training class or convention?

Do you have a lot of crises when you're out of the office?

If you answered yes to most of these questions, not only are you not practicing the biblical example of management, you may find that you're not pleasing your corporate manager either.

According to Everett T. Suters, author of *Succeed in Spite of Yourself*, senior management does not look favorably on the manager who has become irreplaceable. Irreplaceable managers become logjams holding up decisions, activities, and the growth of other employees.

That thought runs contrary to some managers' thinking because many have the wrong concept of delegation. They look on delegation as dumping the undesirable tasks on their subordinates or as shirking their own responsibilities when they don't have time to get them done. Neither is the case.

Delegation, just as in Moses' day, is a means for developing others to their fullest potential in a way that will help everyone reach the desired goal. Women employees seem to have more trouble than men in embracing the value of delegation. Perhaps that's because for so long women were trained to pick up the slack at home for their husbands and children. A child says, "I got a spot on my shirt that I can't get out." Mother responds, "Just leave it in the sink. I'll see what I can do," rather than referring the child to spot removers or other methods she herself will later try.

She is accepting upward delegation from her children; they tell her what she has to get done.

On the job, senior executives do not want to be delegated to in this manner. They prefer that their managers train their subordinates and co-workers to assume the necessary tasks themselves.

So what is good delegation as Moses and Jesus practiced it? Delegating is not simply assigning tasks. An assignment is something like: "Print out copies of the last four years' quarterly reports." Delegating is much broader, leading to the accomplishment of a goal. Researchers have outlined several levels of delegation:

- Look into the situation and bring me the facts and alternatives. I'll make the decision.
- Recommend a decision for my approval.
- Let me know what decision you are making. Do it unless I say not to.
- Take action. Let me know what you did and how it turns out.
- Take action. Let me know only if things didn't work out.
- Take action. You don't need to let me know anything else.

Different parts of the job require different delegation levels. Those managers who stop at the first level are merely assigning tasks; they soon become problems to their organization and everyone concerned.

Here are some *do*s and *don't*s that will improve your delegation habits.

Do pick the right people for the right jobs. Be careful not to give all the ho-hum jobs to one person and those that give a sense of satisfaction and challenge just to the most willing. Assign your people jobs they have been trained to handle.

Do transfer the freedom and authority that go with the task. Instead of outlining all the steps to be taken, simply explain the results you want, the date they're needed, and the acceptable cost: "Please see that all employees who will attend next week's meeting have copies of report A and report B before Wednesday. Keep the printing and shipping costs below three hundred dollars." The employee develops his or her own decision-making skills by determining when, where, and how.

Do be specific about the desired results, including time limits and money. You cannot measure success if you don't make your employees aware of exactly what you want to achieve with the project. Clarify everything. If there are extenuating circumstances and problems, let your employees know from the beginning.

Now for the *don't*s:

Don't demand perfection. You have made mistakes; they will make mistakes. Their occasional mistakes are no reason to throw the whole process of delegation out the window.

Don't accept upward delegation. In effect, employees delegate to their bosses with phrases such as, "I don't know if we should buy Brand X or Brand Y computers for this office. What do you think?" The boss then "puts the monkey on his back" and assumes responsibility for that decision when he could have responded with, "Why don't you investigate both models and come back to me with your recommendation?"

Jesus spent three years preparing His disciples to carry on the ministry that has been growing for the last two thousand years in His earthly absence. Have you spent comparable time in developing your own employees who look to you for leadership?

Irreplaceable is not a compliment.

For Further Reflection:

And the twelve summoned the body of the disciples and said, "It is not right that we should give up preaching the word of God to serve tables. Therefore, brethren, pick out from among you seven men of good repute, full of the Spirit and of wisdom, whom we may appoint to this duty."

Acts 6:2, 3 RSV

12. Feeling Fine: The Daniel Dilemma

Like an athlete I punish my body, treating it roughly, training it to do what it should, not what it wants to. Otherwise I fear that after enlisting others for the race, I myself might be declared unfit and ordered to stand aside.

1 Corinthians 9:27 TLB

It is vain for you to rise up early, to sit up late, to eat the bread of sorrows: for so he giveth his beloved sleep.

Psalms 127:2

You look at your watch, and it's 7:00 P.M. The sentences you're composing for the proposal look like so much mishmash on the yellow legal pad. How can you possibly get it finished, get on the plane tomorrow afternoon to fly to San Francisco, and present it to your biggest prospective customer? Besides that, you're hungry, you're exhausted, and

75

you're guilty of promising your son you'd catch a few throws and then not being home before dark. You begin to feel inefficient. How do other people do it?

They've learned that stamina starts with your attitude. Stamina comes in a controlled way when you learn to break fatiguing habits and learn new ones—ones that keep you fit for both the physical and emotional endurance tests you face on the job.

But, you may ask, doesn't fatigue go with the territory? And don't many people do their best work under pressure? No, to both questions.

Fatigue comes from both psychological and physical sources. As busy employees, we work long hours under emotional pressure. But mental work involves little physical exhaustion; it's the emotional stress of travel, conflicts, decisions, and deadlines that saps our energy.

Fatigue leads to inefficiency, distorted perceptions, lowered standards, poor decisions, loss of initiative, and emotional lows. According to Mortimer R. Feinberg and Aaron Levenstein in their *Wall Street Journal* article "Building Endurance," psychologists noted during World War II that pilots made the most errors as they returned to land after a dangerous raid. The analysts pinpointed the cause as the pilots' tendency at the point of fatigue to relax their standards of performance quality and accuracy. Fatigue does the same to businesspeople, making them unable to judge their slipping performance.

So if fatigue doesn't automatically come with the territory from nine to five, what are its causes? Anger. Failure. Boredom. Poor eating habits. Inadequate exercise. Insufficient sleep. The good news is that all of these can be controlled.

Refuse to carry around emotional baggage such as hostility. Learn to slough off the idea of working with someone you find difficult. If you can't limit your contact with that person, at least psyche yourself up with the thought, "I'm getting paid twenty dollars an hour to work with that person. A little discomfort is worth it."

If you have failed to meet your own expectations, find the

source of that failure and reeducate yourself. Find new resources, new methods, or new goals.

If boredom on the job is the cause, look outside your job for the extra dimension that will recreate excitement and thus energy in your life. Why not work on your spiritual goals if your work gives your mind time to wander? Whom can you minister to? Who needs a helping hand or a listening ear?

The physical causes of fatigue are even easier to correct and control than the emotional causes.

Peter M. Miller, in his book *The Hilton Head Executive Stamina Program*, points out that prolonged mental concentration causes a reduction in muscle glycogen, the blood sugar that serves as stored energy. Our brain is dependent on glucose for mental alertness and stamina. Glucose comes from complex carbohydrates such as fruits, vegetables, breads, cereals, potatoes, and pasta. Our overall diet should contain about 60 percent complex carbohydrates; we need only 15 percent protein.

Now we understand why Daniel (Daniel 1) and his friends were more mentally alert on their simple diet than on the king's rich meats. And notice that Daniel drank only water. The loss of body fluids inside a stuffy, dry office results in lethargy. Fluid loss is even greater when you drink coffee, tea, caffeinated colas, or alcohol.

Power lunches aren't what they used to be. In case you haven't noticed, more and more people are making their midday meals light. The power comes in their mental alertness.

In addition to eating and drinking correctly, we need exercise—at least twenty to thirty minutes every day. You don't have time to exercise? You don't have time *not* to exercise. Exercise keeps you mentally alert so you can accomplish more in less time.

Jess Bell, sixty-three-year-old CEO of Bonnie Bell cosmetics, believes that staying healthy and physically fit is vital to his continued success and that of all his employees (*Small Business Report*, February 1987). Consequently, he maintains a daily exercise routine and has established health and fitness centers at both the company's administrative offices and its manufacturing facility. He claims that the strenuous fitness program required for his hobby of mountain climbing has helped him build the stamina to run his $50 million company. Exercise programs, according to Bell, help foster team spirit, cooperation, and a balanced business and personal life.

Putting his money where his mouth is, Bell encourages his employees to use the exercise facilities by giving them an extra thirty-minute lunch period when exercising. They are allowed to wear casual clothes in the afternoon after their workout. They receive a complimentary breakfast when they participate in the weekly run sponsored by the company. The company also provides financial incentives for employees who exercise, lose weight, or quit smoking. Staying in top physical condition is top priority.

If even the corporate world realizes the value of physical fitness, shouldn't Christians be leading the pack?

The writer of Ecclesiastes noted that the race is not always to the swift. The real test is to keep on running.

For Further Reflection:

I beseech you therefore, brethren, by the mercies of God, that ye present your bodies a living sacrifice, holy, acceptable unto God, which is your reasonable service.

Romans 12:1

Beloved, I wish above all things that thou mayest prosper and be in health, even as thy soul prospereth.

3 John 2

13. Are Leaders Born or Does God Create Them on the Job?

For the leaders of this people cause them to err; and they that are led of them are destroyed.

Isaiah 9:16

Where are the future leaders of corporate America, a correspondent to Ann Landers recently (December 21, 1986) wanted to know. Warren Bennis, widely acclaimed management consultant and professor in the School of Business Administration at the University of Southern California, responded to the inquirer:

> Japan, which is about the size of Montana, supports 115 million people. The largest automobile manufacturer in the world is not General Motors, it is Toyota.
> Eight of the 10 largest banks in the world (in terms of assets) are in Japan. (Citicorp, the only American bank on the list, is third.)

> In Japan, students attend school 240 days a year as compared with 180 days in the United States. . . . Ninety-seven percent of Japan's students finish high school. In Chicago, it's about 50 percent, and about half of those who do finish cannot read at a high school level. The illiteracy rate in Japan is less than 1 percent. Ours is about 27 percent.
>
> The Japanese value their young people and their elderly. Strong emphasis is placed on education and family. Respect for teachers and parents is deeply embedded in their culture.

Bennis concludes that we have little to fear from the Japanese model but much to learn.

If the Bible teaches anything about leadership, it teaches that leaders are made. Businesspeople can learn to lead those around them to meet corporate goals as well as God's goals for their lives.

At the beginning of his career, Moses had no experience, a sinful past (he'd murdered an Egyptian), no authority over or respect from the people ("the people won't listen to me, Lord"), and at least one serious weakness in his job skills (his stammering speech). All he had were connections. God had provided for his upbringing in the palace by pharaoh's daughter, but those connections didn't bring Moses his success in leading God's people to the Promised Land. Moses *learned* to lead.

The disciples are yet another example of what God does with men who are willing to become leaders. With little money and less political acumen, they turned the first-century world upside down.

So what does it take to be a real leader who serves God and the corporation?

Leaders are idea people. They don't necessarily run with the crowd; they turn the crowd. They focus on what to do and when to do it, not whom to blame for trouble or inaction.

Leaders take risks. They look at the possible rewards and confidently take action. They do not tie their egos to possible failure, so they can help others learn from their mistakes.

Leaders develop their followers. Army Chief of Staff General George C. Marshall advised his colleagues to make their subordinates self-reliant: "If you want a man to be for you, never let him feel he is dependent on you. Make him feel you are in some way dependent on him." Leaders learn their employees' strengths and appreciate them for those abilities. They find ways to praise and reward them and push them to develop their potential in their weak areas. They are clear in their directions, firm with their goals and procedures.

In leading people to attain their highest potential, leaders keep them informed, give them purpose, and generate excitement about the tasks to be completed. They shine the spotlight on their staff performers and let them know what it feels like to be on the front edge of success—in the small things as well as the big things. Leaders generate energy for and urgency about a job well done.

Leaders take the time to get to know their people personally. They are available to them, they listen to their questions, they are sensitive to their disappointments and fears. They let them be humans, not machines.

Does such sensitivity make a difference in followers' attitudes? You bet. An accountant for a large oil company recently told me, "I've resigned my job and will be leaving next week. Frankly, I'm very good at what I do. My boss knows it, and he sends everybody else in the department to me for help with their work. But I never get any recognition for what I do. All the reports I prepare are for his signature, and I'm tired of making him look literate. I'm tired of carrying his lunch."

Leaders are always around to give support. Leaders are not hit-and-run delegators. They do not dump an assignment and leave a subordinate to sink or swim without providing appropriate psychological support for the completion of the task. In other words, the development of a subordinate does not mean finding someone to blame in case things go wrong; it means finding someone to praise when things go right.

Finally, leaders draw others to them because they model the attitudes that others respect and expect. They capitalize on their strengths and find others to cover their weaknesses.

Learn to be that leader United States corporations need so desperately. Look for opportunities to turn into ideas, be willing to take risks for rewards, and develop subordinates to their fullest potential, making them feel significant and offering support. When you consider Moses' forty years of apprenticeship in the wilderness, it's not too late to start your own leadership-learning curve.

For Further Reflection:

When there is moral rot within a nation, its government topples easily; but with honest, sensible leaders there is stability.

Proverbs 28:2 TLB

With good men in authority, the people rejoice; but with the wicked in power, they groan. . . . A just king gives stability to his nation, but one who demands bribes destroys it.

Proverbs 29:2, 4 TLB

And Moses said unto God, Who am I, that I should go unto Pharaoh, and that I should bring forth the children of Israel out of Egypt? And he said, Certainly I will be with thee; and this shall be a token unto thee, that I have sent thee: When thou hast brought forth the people out of Egypt, ye shall serve God upon this mountain.

Exodus 3:11, 12

14. Contented Cows and Curdled Milk

Not that I speak in respect of want: for I have learned, in whatsoever state I am, therewith to be content. I know both how to be abased, and I know how to abound: every where and in all things I am instructed both to be full and to be hungry, both to abound and to suffer need. I can do all things through Christ which strengtheneth me.

Philippians 4:11–13

But godliness with contentment is great gain.

1 Timothy 6:6

Therefore do not be anxious about tomorrow, for tomorrow will be anxious for itself. Let the day's own trouble be sufficient for the day.

Matthew 6:34 RSV

Is contentment anathema to business? According to many employees and employers, it is. *INC* recently ran a feature story by the sole proprietor of a small landscape service. Friends were constantly after him to expand his business. But to do so, the owner would have had to go heavily into debt to finance the equipment necessary to handle larger commercial accounts and hire more staff. He expressed deep satisfaction at handling only residential accounts, because he got to know his customers and was able to take time to get involved, in small ways, with their lives. He concluded that he was making enough money to provide well for his family and that was his goal. As a result, he had few pressures on the job and a lot of time with his family and friends.

His attitude and management style seem to be an anomaly to the entrepreneur. But according to the letters written to the editor, this man's contentment and sense of satisfaction proved highly refreshing to the readers. There was and is much to be said for contentment with the status quo.

Contrary to popular belief, "doing without" is not the major cause of discontent; often the problem is doing with more. The more we have, the more we want. We have been swept into the world's concern for "getting." When our needs are met, we start on our want list.

Is that all bad? Weren't we taught to better ourselves and that each generation of parents should want better things for its children? Yes. But we've learned the lesson too well. We've scaled the wall of improvement and jumped into the lake of discontent: We're drowning in the depths of indebtedness. Instead of following the biblical admonition to owe no man, we owe every man. We have lost our sense of values, confusing the price of a good pair of jeans for an autographed label. We've misplaced our priorities, often putting work before worship and family. We're suffering from misguided giving, confusing our tip to the taxi driver with our tithe for God.

English clergyman Charles Caleb Colton noted that "True contentment depends not on what we have; a tub was large enough for Diogenes, but a world was too little for Alexander."

Discontent is like paint splattered over a once clean windowpane. It mars the view so the whole place looks vacant, as though it were under construction.

Older employees long for the energy and good health of young new stars on the corporate track; young employees long for the experience and the contacts of the older. The powerful administrator longs for the peace of mind of the staff member; the staff member longs for the clout of the boss. The wealthy long for safety from thieves and charlatan investment advisers; the poor wish for the financial security of the rich.

True contentment is an attitude, even an active, creative attitude. Someone has observed that the contented man is never poor, while the discontented is never rich. Perhaps we need a new pair of eyes for our bank balance, work, people, and conditions around us. Contentment leads us to massage a situation until we get everything from it that God has for us.

If you can't get overtime hours and wages, can you use the spare time to develop a stronger relationship with your family or friends? If you can't transfer to a new job and learn a new skill, can you learn new and better ways to do the old job? If your job provides no challenge, and therefore no pressure, can you put your energies into a volunteer project in the church or community?

Although we should never be satisfied with what we are, we should always be satisfied with what we have. And if you can't honestly say that you've arrived at contentment, don't give up on developing that attitude. The Apostle Paul assured us that he had *learned* contentment. Praise God for what you have, and trust Him for what you need and what you feel.

For Further Reflection:

Two things have I required of thee; deny me them not before I die: Remove far from me vanity and lies; give me

neither poverty nor riches; feed me with food convenient
for me: Lest I be full, and deny thee, and say, Who is the
Lord? or lest I be poor, and steal, and take the name of my
God in vain.

Proverbs 30:7–9

Let your conversation be without covetousness; and be
content with such things as ye have: for he hath said, I will
never leave thee, nor forsake thee.

Hebrews 13:5

And the soldiers likewise demanded of him, saying, And
what shall we do? And he said unto them, Do violence to
no man, neither accuse any falsely; and be content with
your wages.

Luke 3:14

The Lord does not let the righteous go hungry, but he
thwarts the craving of the wicked.

Proverbs 10:3 RSV

But my God shall supply all your need according to his
riches in glory by Christ Jesus.

Philippians 4:19

And the peace of God, which passeth all understanding,
shall keep your hearts and minds through Christ Jesus.

Philippians 4:7

15. Right and Stupid

If a godly man compromises with the wicked, it is like polluting a fountain or muddying a spring.

Proverbs 25:26 TLB

The executive vice-president of a large software company asked me about obtaining a free preview of a computer-based sales training program distributed by my company. I was a little shocked at the request, because his company has a competitive software package on the market.

But he explained this way: "Oh, yeah, I'm still vice-president at XYZ Company. But headquarters is out of state, and they don't even know what I'm doing down here. Actually, a few months ago, I began my own consulting business. And I've got a client overseas who wants to buy sales training. If your sales package is better than ours, I've no qualms about recommending your program to my client. I'm leaving Company XYZ in the next few months, anyway."

I sent him the free preview package. Several weeks later, on his new consulting business letterhead, he returned the sales package, saying he had decided to recommend another one to his client. At my last contact with him two years after that, he was *still* vice-president of XYZ Company. And he was still operating a consulting business on somebody else's payroll!

Do businesspeople not hear daily about such unethical things? Certainly, and even much worse. Lying, cheating, murder, drugs, tax scams, abuse, and evil abound these days. We still *talk* about such things, but what has changed is our way of *thinking* about such things.

"Greed is all right, by the way. I want you to know that. I think greed is healthy. You can be greedy and still feel good about yourself" (*Newsweek*, December 1, 1986). This statement from Ivan F. Boesky, part of his 1985 commencement address to the School of Business Administration at the University of California, Berkeley, was greeted with laughter and applause! That's right—agreement with and admiration for the chief perpetrator of the biggest insider trading scandal to date on Wall Street.

When we referred to such unethical practices in the past, we used words like *wrong*. Today, we substitute nicer terms. Meg Greenfield, in her *Newsweek* column (July 28, 1986) very perceptively identifies five new ways of thinking about *wrong*. To elaborate on her labels:

Right and Stupid

This term is used with openers such as, "I just can't believe he did that; it was so stupid. Surely, he knew he would be caught when. . . . " Watergate, Gary Hart, and the Boesky Wall Street scandal serve as good (or bad) examples. Journalists explained to us not that Hart's behavior was morally wrong, but that he "handled things" badly.

Right and Not Necessarily Unconstitutional

This term has a flip-flop meaning that implies since the wrong was not mentioned specifically in the Constitution or the Bible, it is morally acceptable. As in, "What do you mean, I can't do that? Where in the Bible does it say . . . ?" As an example of this reasoning, consider the corporate take-over game. According to Roger Smith, General Motors CEO: "We have got to watch the corporate raiders. They destroy equity. They destroy jobs. They destroy communities. All for their own gain. That's not right and it should not be allowed in America. Legitimate takeovers OK. Corporate raiders for their own profit, no good" (*Newsweek*, December 1, 1986).

We're forever telling our representatives in Congress to legislate against things that are "right" but unconstitutional, which would never have even entered the minds of our fore-fathers back when they still had *wrong* in their vocabulary.

Right and Sick

This term is used for wrong behavior that is now consid-ered a mental or physical ailment, such as homosexuality or alcoholism. The "sick" person has no personal, moral re-sponsibility to control his behavior. As in: "I just can't help myself. I need your understanding and patience."

Have you considered the implications of the drunk-driving campaigns being shown on TV? The pitch is, if you're really a good friend, why would you let your drunk buddy crawl behind the wheel of a car? Why don't you take his keys away? While we would all agree that drunks shouldn't be on the road, since when has the responsibility shifted from the drunk to his friend? "Right and sick" has boiled down to, "He was under such pressure. . . ."

Right and Only to Be Expected

As in: "Well, she asked for it. Why in the world would she leave the money in an unlocked desk drawer?" Does oppor-tunity make the thief? We have turned victims into perpe-trators of wrong and the guilty into opportunists.

Right and Complex

This term probably substitutes most often in the corporate setting, although we hear it, too, in official government explanations about such things as the Iran-Contra situation. As in: "Yes, normally, we hesitate to engage in that sort of thing, but there are extenuating circumstances here. The situation is very complex."

Whatever happened to *wrong*?

Frankly, for most of us, the term *wrong* involves too much effort of the will. According to Oscar Wilde: "The only way to get rid of a temptation is to yield to it." Oh, it doesn't take much to say no when we're praying in church or meeting with Christian friends and associates. Eschewed reasoning usually strikes us when we're in the middle of a merger meeting, filling out expense accounts, or designing direct-mail pieces.

Some of us pray for help with our moral choices and then rush into morally questionable situations. The result is much like stuffing ourselves with high-calorie junk foods and then praying we don't gain weight.

Therefore, the time and place for a proper perspective on moral boundaries is before we see the figures on the business plan, before we talk to the lawyer about the foggy new clause to be inserted, and before we hear what the competitor has planned.

True temptation is when we have opportunity and our will is all that restrains us. Ask not: Is it legal? Is it defensible? Is it understandable? Instead, ask: Is it morally responsible? Is it morally right? Is it simply stupid and **wrong?**

For Further Reflection:

Finally, brethren, whatsoever things are true, whatsoever things are honest, whatsoever things are just, whatsoever things are pure, whatsoever things are lovely, whatsoever things are of good report; if there be any virtue, and if there be any praise, think on these things.

Philippians 4:8

16. The Work Ethic Versus the Workaholic

For even when we were with you, this we commanded you, that if any would not work, neither should he eat.

2 Thessalonians 3:10

It is in vain that you rise up early and go late to rest, eating the bread of anxious toil; for he gives to his beloved sleep.

Psalms 127:2 RSV

We generally find people hold one of two extreme attitudes about work. First, there are those who think of it as Adam's curse, a grind, drudgery, something unpleasant stuck between the weekends. But nevertheless, as a necessary part of their right to live and "their fair share," they work to provide for themselves and family.

Then there is the second attitude about work—those who

love their work and find a great sense of fulfillment from it. In their minds, man was put on earth to achieve. They have found true happiness and true freedom in being able to do work they love and make an adequate living doing it.

Workaholics come from both camps. Some are compelled by the work ethic and a sense of a curse, doom, and duty. Others are motivated by love of the work itself.

A few years ago, workaholism was in favor and often dismissed with a wink. Frequently magazines and newspapers carried quizzes that told you if you were becoming a workaholic. If you "failed" the test and proved to be a borderline or full-fledged workaholic, you came away feeling good about yourself. You were going beyond the call of duty; you were committed; you were a superachiever.

I began to rethink that skewed idea a few years back, after a long walk with my parents. On one of their visits to my home, we were all strolling along under the tall pines at dusk when my parents began to reminisce about my childhood. After we'd gone through the days of my brother and I working in the cotton fields and my usual weekly household chores, we began to talk finances. My dad remarked, "We sure didn't have any money back then. I couldn't send you to college, and I didn't teach you much. But I guess the one thing your mother and I taught you was to work." Then he smiled, but with a very serious look in his eye. "The thing is, I think you learned that lesson too well."

You see, I'd just been advised that I had to have major surgery right away, surgery that would require a long recuperation time. And I had decided that I must put it off because I simply didn't have time. I had travel and speaking engagements, the seminar business, two books under contract, Christmas coming up, and the family; you get the picture.

The Bible never intended it to be so. God rested. He commanded us to rest. I began to give my attitude and what was happening in my life more serious thought. If a little work is good, isn't more work better?

No. For several reasons.

First, we soon find that the six days God gave us to do our work isn't enough. We're scrambling to squeeze a little more onto the agenda, and it spills over into Sunday. You know, the little things: reading professional journals and other job-related materials, balancing the checkbooks, paying the bills, buying the groceries, painting the spare bedroom. And the first thing you know, we're breaking God's commandment to keep His day holy.

Second, we find that our work crowds God's work out. We find less and less time to worship, to minister to others, to spend in personal Bible study and prayer.

Third, work begins to crowd out the family. You miss more dinners together. You attend fewer worship services together. You talk less. The Apostle Paul insisted that the man who doesn't take care of his own family is worse than the heathen. Many of us interpret that care almost exclusively in terms of finances, so we stay at the office longer and work harder. But how about taking care of our family's emotional needs—their need of our time, attention, communication, presence, energy, and sensitivity?

Fourth, work begins to crowd out friends and makes us a very limited, unbalanced, and often boring person. When was the last time you went out to dinner with someone not associated with you through work? When was the last time you had a serious conversation about new ideas, about new trends, about the world, about art or literature or music, about spiritual matters?

Fifth, overwork can build hostility among your colleagues on the job. Do your colleagues slip in later than you or go home earlier, leaving you breathing fire down the hall about their lack of commitment or accomplishments? The workaholic has little or no patience with others who don't work as long and as hard as he or she does. In fact, the workaholic even works harder to make up for others' "lack of commitment." Most employees can't sustain the workaholic's long hours; therefore, the workaholic breeds hostility and antagonism when used as a model or the standard for performance.

The sixth problem with workaholics is that their own performance slips. Don't confuse high energy levels and long hours with results. Samuel Butler observes, "To do great work a man must be very idle as well as very industrious." Just as a machine gets less efficient as its parts wear out, so the workaholic gets less efficient without rest and refueling. When was the last time you simply cleared your mind of work and let it float free? When was the last time you had a completely new, exciting idea, one that gave you food for thought for as many pleasurable hours as a good book?

Finally, workaholics may be working to cover up emotional pain and problems that need to be dealt with rather than submerged on the job. If work is a medicine, it's often not the most effective cure. It's like taking an aspirin for a fever without getting an antibiotic to kill the infection. Sooner or later the real disease will surface and take its toll on your job, your family, or your own mental well-being.

Work is good, right, and God's plan for our lives. Too much work is not better; it's harmful to all concerned. Are you reading this book at midnight or 5:00 A.M.? Why?

For Further Reflection:

She looketh well to the ways of her household, and eateth not the bread of idleness.

Proverbs 31:27

And to Adam he said, "Because you have listened to the voice of your wife, and have eaten of the tree of which I commanded you, 'You shall not eat of it,' cursed is the ground because of you; in toil you shall eat of it all the days of your life."

Genesis 3:17 RSV

17. Time Management and Creation of the Six-Day Workweek

Let all things be done decently and in order.

1 Corinthians 14:40

So teach us to number our days, that we may apply our hearts unto wisdom.

Psalms 90:12

Do you ever feel like standing up from your desk in the middle of the afternoon, blowing a loud whistle, and shouting "Freeze"? Unfortunately, the command wouldn't help, because there's no such thing as a real time-out. If you lose your money, you can start over to accumulate more. If you lose your health, you can often be healed or accommodated. If you forget things, you can relearn them. If you lose friends, you can apologize and restore them or make new ones. If you lose your good reputation, you can rebuild it by contrition and effort. Many of God's gifts, such as grace, mercy, and love, are continuous.

Only time is limited; you can never recapture or rebuild it. But most of us lack a healthy respect for time, for its benefits, and for its losses. In fact, we sometimes even have a vague concept of its passing. Have you ever noticed that when your favorite team is winning, a two-hour game seems but a couple of minutes? And when you're mowing the grass, two minutes drags by like two hours!

Respect for time and a true perspective of its value can be powerful motivators for redeeming the time that remains, as long as we stop whining about the lack of it and stop wasting it.

A few years back, when I thought myself too busy to exercise, a CEO of a locally headquartered corporation hired me to ghostwrite a book for him. In the course of our writing project, I was forced to give up the idea that I was too busy to exercise when I heard his exercise schedule: three lunch hours a week at the local club, a late-night hour of tennis twice a week, a Saturday morning of horseback riding or golf. Plus he is an active deacon in his church, spends time at the Star of Hope Mission he helped found, and enjoys time with his active wife, children, and grandchildren. There went my exercise excuses, along with the notion that executives don't have adequate time for the important things in life.

National Liberty Corporation, which owns several insurance companies and affiliated marketing and service organizations nationwide, had as its chairman–founder Arthur S. DeMoss until his death in 1979. He was a pioneer in the mass marketing of life and health insurance and earned a prominent place in the history of insurance in this country. Arthur DeMoss had this to say about the management of time after his spiritual conversion (*God's Secrets of Success*, 1980, page 67):

In my own experience, the matter of time had been even more pressing than the money problem. It seemed that eighty hours a week were not sufficient even for the needs of the business, let alone finding time for Christian activity. Again I want to testify to the glory of God that the more time I have given Him the more He has given me in return. Now He has permitted and privileged me to spend almost as much time on His business as I used to devote to my own.

Charles H. Spurgeon agreed about the foolishness of mismanaging time: "He who rushes from his bed to his business without first spending time with God is as foolish as though he had not washed or dressed, and as unwise as one dashing to battle without arms or armor."

If you need a checklist to determine how well you manage your time, try this one:

- Are you becoming more forgetful lately? Do you forget to return telephone calls? To keep appointments, or even to set them? To buy gifts or send cards or notes for birthdays and anniversaries?
- Do you have a cluttered desk? Things out of place and tasks half finished indicate a cluttered mind and cluttered time.
- Do you find yourself doing trivial, nonproductive things, such as considering a new color ink for your memo pads? Such things are often desperate attempts to "at least get something done."
- Are you at odds with your co-workers, your friends, and your family? Are they nagging you about missing their deadlines, about not doing the report right, about not spending enough time with them?
- Has your time alone with God in prayer and Bible study become negotiable? Maybe you do, and maybe you don't?
- Do you have a free-floating sour attitude about your job, yourself, and the world in general? When we don't feel as though we're accomplishing something of value and en-

joying the quality of our lives, we tend to blame others, ourselves, time, and circumstances.

Maybe you see the symptoms of mismanaged time in your life. What should you do? As with other things, follow Jesus' example. Like us at the office, He was frequently interrupted on the job. He had the sick stop Him in the street and ask for healing. He had close friends call on Him in time of grief and ask for comfort and His physical presence. Just as we have new employees to train, He had disciples to question and teach. In short, His time, like ours, was not always His own.

But He managed. He spent time with His family and friends at their important occasions, He spent time alone with God, and He accomplished His mission on earth.

So how did He do it? First, with preparation: He spent thirty years of His life preparing for the last three, and He never quit preparing. Even the week of His death, He still sent His disciples ahead to find His transportation and to prepare the upper room for His last lesson to them. How could He afford not to prepare for important occasions such as these?

Preparation. How much time do we spend going off half-cocked and then cleaning up the mess? How much time do we spend redoing projects because we didn't gather our resources and prepare things correctly the first time around? How much time do we spend repairing damaged relationships because we didn't prepare before plunging?

Second, focus. He focused on what was important and what was within range of His mission. He didn't spend much time collecting worldly possessions, but He spent a lot of time with those who stopped Him for physical and spiritual healing.

Without focus, our minds and our businesses will self-destruct. How much time do we spend arranging and attending meetings that have little to do with real progress or results? How much time do we spend doing second-, third-, and fourth-priority items while our number-one priority is waiting for us? How many days, weeks, or months do we drift through without ever setting clear goals for our accomplishment?

Third, delegation. Jesus delegated the less important chores. Do you remember that the Twelve picked up the leftover baskets of bread and fish on the hillside? Many of us can't delegate because we haven't done the first two things—prepare and focus. That is, we haven't taught and prepared our subordinates to do the quality of work we expect. We haven't focused on our mission far enough ahead to know what needs to be done and when it needs to be done to reach our goal.

If the Scripture teaches us anything about time, it teaches accountability. Take a good accounting of the wasted time around your office during the next few days. Someone has said that killing time is not murder; it's suicide.

For Further Reflection:

He who tills his land will have plenty of bread, but he who follows worthless pursuits has no sense.

Proverbs 12:11 RSV

A son who gathers in summer is prudent, but a son who sleeps in harvest brings shame.

Proverbs 10:5 RSV

See then that ye walk circumspectly, not as fools, but as wise, Redeeming the time, because the days are evil. Wherefore be ye not unwise, but understanding what the will of the Lord is.

Ephesians 5:15–17

18. The Craze to Advertise Ourselves

Finally, brethren, whatever is true, whatever is honorable, whatever is just, whatever is pure, whatever is lovely, whatever is gracious, if there is any excellence, if there is anything worthy of praise, think about these things.

Philippians 4:8 RSV

Only in our society could the refusal to advertise ourselves be considered arrogance. An actor who doesn't want to tour to promote his movie gets a shove from the producers and a thumbed nose from the general public. We seem to be saying, "Just who do you think you are? You're not *that* well-known that you can take our accolades and our money for granted."

Joey Adams points out the difference between an actor and a civilian: When the civilian's house burns down, he calls his insurance agent; when an actor's house burns down, he calls his press agent.

Not only has the craze washed over the stars and starlets, but it also has splashed over into the corporate scene.

- "Lose from six to thirty inches the first day." Did someone double dare them to make that promise?
- "Another of our best-selling authors brings you. . . ." Did you ever wonder how they could all be best-sellers and still virtually unheard of by the general public?

I'm not about to insist advertising is unbiblical or that your business stop advertising its product or service. In fact, we as Christians probably need to do more in advertising our faith and lifting Jesus up so He can draw men to Himself. Instead, I'm attempting to reconcile the biblical admonitions toward humility and this craze to advertise ourselves.

And to advertise deceptively, at that! Retailers often have three sets of sales figures for their newest product: the numbers they give the public, the numbers they really sold, and the numbers they give the IRS.

Philippians 4:8 would be a good place to start when we meet with our PR staff. Is it true? Is your advertising completely, utterly, wholly true? "Best-selling" compared to what measure? The "largest" in what way? Can your claims be verified? By whom? What are you *not* telling the consumer, and why?

Is it honorable? Does your advertisement encourage people to their benefit? If questioned, would you like your personal name linked to the slogan, photo, or campaign? Would you be willing to go on television and accept responsibility for how this product changed an individual's life-style or benefited society as a whole?

Is it just? Does it leave the true impression about your competitors? Would you like your competitors to use the same tactics against you? Are your ads asking the age-old question, "When did you stop beating your wife?"

Is it pure? In your own way, are you using sex to sell soap?

Are your ads blatantly vulgar and immoral? Will your ads lead the consumer toward or away from a godly life?

With those stringent questions, how would you ever advertise anything successfully?

Try honesty and directness. How do you respond to a direct-mail letter that begins, "Would you like to make a million dollars in the next six months?" Throw it away? So do most people, as I've found from questioning them in sales-writing workshops. And if somehow readers get tricked into reading to the bottom of page two ("So all you have to do is send us $99.95, and we'll send you our cassette tape telling you how to make your million dollars"), they get angry. They feel baited or "had." Few people respond well to that kind of come-on.

Don't underestimate the value of being forthright with your advertising message.

Isaac Newton said of his own accomplishments: "I do not know what I may appear to the world; but to myself I seem to have been only like a boy playing on the seashore, and diverting myself in now and then finding a smoother pebble or a prettier shell than ordinary, whilst the great ocean of truth lay all undiscovered before me."

Quality work speaks for itself. Customers and colleagues often make the best and most effective references for our prospective clients and bosses.

When I was beginning my own practice, I once heard a nationally known and highly regarded management consultant respond to a question from the audience about how he promoted himself and got so well-known. His answer: "I hide, and they always seem to find me somehow."

Before advertising yourself, your product, or your service, check the previous list once again: Is it true? Is it just? Is it honorable? Is it pure?

The old saying that if we build a better mousetrap everyone will beat a path to our door is, of course, not always true. But I do think it's true more often than we businesspeople think. At the very least, shouldn't we as Christians make sure our mousetrap advertising is clear and honorable?

For Further Reflection:

Let another man praise thee, and not thine own mouth; a stranger, and not thine own lips.

Proverbs 27:2

But the meek shall possess the land, and delight themselves in abundant prosperity.

Psalms 37:11 RSV

The reward for humility and fear of the Lord is riches and honor and life.

Proverbs 22:4 RSV

19. Advisers With a Bigger Briefcase and a Long-Distance Phone Number

---

Without counsel purposes are disappointed: but in the multitude of counsellors they are established.

Proverbs 15:22

When Harry Truman assumed the presidency at the death of Roosevelt, Speaker of the House Sam Rayburn let Truman in on a little secret: "From here on out you're going to have lots of people around you. They'll try to put a wall around you and cut you off from any ideas but theirs. They'll tell you what a great man you are, Harry. But you and I both know you ain't" (*Bits and Pieces*).

Even with a blow like that to the jaw of pride, few businesspeople would deny their need for good, sound advice. In his book *Think and Grow Rich*, Dr. Napoleon Hill tells us that Thomas Edison, Henry Ford, and Harvey Firestone were all close friends who consulted one another, often going off

104

on retreats together to share ideas and develop solutions to problems. If these great minds needed advice, what about the rest of us?

But need doesn't motivate us all. "Many a man wins glory for prudence by seeking advice, then seeking advice as to what advice would be best to take, and finally following appetite," observed American physician Austin O'Malley. And according to eighteenth-century wit Samuel Johnson, "Advice is seldom welcome. Those who need it most like it least."

Those two short observations just about cover all the problems inherent with advice. We often have our minds made up before we seek advice. We get too many opinions, and then we don't know which to follow. When we really need advice, we don't like what we hear.

Let's look more closely at the first—having our minds made up before we seek advice. King Jehoshaphat of Judah (2 Chronicles 18) suffered from that malady. When King Ahab of Israel asked him to make an alliance and go to war against the Syrians to recapture their city of Ramoth-gilead, Jehoshaphat gave his answer before asking God what He thought of the idea! In effect, he said to King Ahab, "My men are your men. Let's go. Oh, by the way, maybe we'd better call in some counselors and check with the Lord." When he didn't get the answer he wanted from God's prophet Micaiah, Ahab threw Micaiah in prison and went to battle anyway, and to his death.

Check yourself: How often do you really only want praise under the guise of advice?

"What do you think about this proposal?" you ask a colleague.

"Looks good," the friend answers. "But there are a couple of issues not addressed here. You might want to consider mentioning the heavy equipment the contractor will need for the job."

Your smile fades into a frown, you reclaim the proposal

and lumber off to your office, convinced that your colleague is jealous because he didn't reel in the client.

Sometimes we don't reject advice because it's too difficult or not what we want to hear; we sometimes reject it because it's too *simple*, too obvious. Such was the case with Naaman, the commander-in-chief of the Syrian army, who sought a cure for his leprosy (2 Kings 5). He thought he had a big problem on his hands. Taking the trouble to get a letter of introduction from his king and load himself with plenty of gifts, he went with great fanfare to the king of Israel for healing by the prophet Elisha. Elisha didn't get too excited about his arrival; he merely sent a messenger out to tell Naaman to go wash himself in the Jordan River seven times to be healed.

So was Naaman thrilled that the solution was so easy? No. His response was to stalk away angrily. It was only when his own servants reasoned with him that he had a change of heart. If the prophet had told you to do something very difficult, wouldn't you have done it? they asked. So what's your hang-up simply because the advice is so easy to take? Finally persuaded, Naaman followed the advice and was healed.

Almost all of us from time to time succumb to the urge to call in an adviser with a bigger briefcase and a long-distance phone number. But why call in a consultant when your secretary gives you a plausible explanation and feasible solution? The proper mind-set for advice is an open mind—even when the advice sounds simple.

The second problem, as we mentioned earlier, is getting too many opinions or getting them from the wrong people. Most of the advice we get is largely our own; people know only as much about the situation as we've told them, and we almost always let them know the answer we want. Beware of those who feed you back your own advice and always echo the majority opinion.

Somehow we gravitate toward the people who don't know any more about the issues than we do. Although Proverbs 14:7 cautions us not to take advice from fools, fools don't always go around wearing tags identifying themselves as such. A good screening question to an adviser might be the cynic's query, "If you're so smart, why ain't you rich?" To what extent has the adviser taken his own advice and proven it to be accurate, appropriate, or effective?

Consider the Old Testament account of Rehoboam and his young friends (2 Chronicles 10). After King Solomon's death, his young, inexperienced son Rehoboam was crowned. As early as his inauguration, he was forced into a decision-making mode. The citizens came to him complaining of what a hard taskmaster his father had been. Just how did he intend to reign over them? they asked. What was his philosophy of government? So new King Rehoboam first went to his older, more experienced advisers. "They'll serve you faithfully the rest of your life," they advised, "if you treat them well."

But Rehoboam refused their advice and went to his young buddies. "Treat them rough and show them who's boss," they advised. Rehoboam had no more than gotten his philosophy stated over the loudspeaker when all but one tribe of his would-be kingdom deserted him.

There's no virtue in asking for a lot of advice from people who know no more than you. Is it pride that inhibits us from seeking out those brighter and more successful than we are and tapping the benefits of their experience?

Finally, in seeking out many counselors, we often hear from the people who have something personal at stake in our decision. Ahab found out the hard way (1 Kings 21). When he complained to his wife, Jezebel, that his real estate deal with Naboth was on hold, Jezebel told him she knew just what to do. Not to worry, she assured him as she arranged to have Naboth killed and then presented her husband the property that Naboth had refused to sell him. We can only imagine that it wasn't purely unselfish love for her husband that created such passion to arrange the land deal!

The best advisers are those who, in addition to being wiser than we are, have no stake in the outcome. They have no horn of their own to blow, no career path to chart, no pocketbook to line.

What kind of advisers should we choose? Not "yes" men and women. And not necessarily our friends and peers. But rather those wiser than ourselves, who share our ultimate values, who have no hope of personal profit from our decisions.

To keep from getting your own advice, be specific about the kind of advice you want. Do you want new ideas and alternatives that you haven't considered? Do you want additional information from the adviser? Do you want insight into how to think through or analyze the facts you have? Finally, stifle the urge to react too quickly, but rather ponder what you hear.

Of course, there's still the biggest problem of all with advice: hearing advice we don't want. As others have noted, if at first you don't succeed, you'll get a lot of advice.

We often denigrate such unsolicited advice. Most of us react to advice that puts us in a bad light or goes against our desires just as King Amaziah did (2 Chronicles 25): "Since when have I asked your advice?" Most of us, however, would do better to follow King David's example. Although David committed grave wrongs, when the prophet Nathan came—unsolicited—to reveal them to him, he listened and repented of his ways.

To paraphrase the proverbs: There is safety in wise counselors who feel free to give us the best advice—whether it's what we want to hear or not.

For Further Reflection:

Where no counsel is, the people fall: but in the multitude of counsellors there is safety.

Proverbs 11:14

Hear counsel, and receive instruction, that thou mayest be wise in thy latter end.

Proverbs 19:20

Though good advice lies deep within a counselor's heart, the wise man will draw it out.

Proverbs 20:5 TLB

Pride leads to arguments; be humble, take advice and become wise.

Proverbs 13:10 TLB

The way of a fool is right in his own eyes: but he that hearkeneth unto counsel is wise.

Proverbs 12:15

Poverty and shame shall be to him that refuseth instruction: but he that regardeth reproof shall be honoured.

Proverbs 13:18

20. Affairs of State— And of the Office

Ye have heard that it was said by them of old time,
Thou shalt not commit adultery: But I say unto you,
That whosoever looketh on a woman to lust after her
hath committed adultery with her already in his
heart.

Matthew 5:27, 28

"Sex has become one of the most discussed subjects of modern times," observed American Catholic Bishop Fulton J. Sheen. "The Victorians pretended it did not exist; the moderns pretend that nothing else exists."

Sexual interest and affairs in the office are not hidden for long. Someone who is not in the chain of command suddenly begins to show up at meetings beside the higher-ranking lover, knowing nothing about the meeting topic and caring less. Suddenly someone is personally delivering all his or her reports, memos, or telephone messages. Someone is staying later and later after hours. Someone with an open-door policy suddenly has it closed too often.

Do companies care? If we are to believe all the management publications and interviews, yes. Mortimer R. Feinberg, chairman of BFS Psychological Associates of New York, and Aaron Levenstein, retired professor at Baruch College, surveyed a small sampling of managers to verify that impression. Out of their 112 respondents, 76 replied that people in their organizations had been asked by their bosses to "observe caution"; 50 managers said that warnings had been issued to discontinue the relationship; 12 reported that those involved in an affair had been denied a promotion; 20 managers reported that some action, including dismissal, had been taken because of the affair.

Why has management taken such a strong stand? Because of the legal headaches involved, for one thing. Corporations are hesitant to infringe on the personal lives of their employees, but at the same time, they are held liable for sexual harassment on the job. Walking the line between knowing of an affair and not knowing of an affair is rather difficult and can be quite costly in court.

Corporations are also concerned about the work performance and productivity of the individuals involved. If an adulterous affair leads to a marriage and family breakup, the employee's performance usually slips. Additionally, how much work time is wasted in flirtatious chitchat on the phone and in secretly meeting the other party during the workday?

Third, management is concerned about the leaking of confidences from one department or situation to another via lover-to-lover shared secrets.

Additionally, there are cries of favoritism and petty jealousies when one is promoted or allowed special privileges because of the rank of the other person in the relationship. An employee having an affair creates tension and puts pressure on his morally upright co-workers. They see him or her getting away with things (for a time) and begin to think they are missing out, that perhaps their own straight theology, philosophy, and moral codes are incorrect. Thus, the conflict and contention intensify among workers on the job.

It's easy to see why management disapproves of office affairs.

Sometimes it's *not* so easy for the involved individuals to see the dangers, both physical and spiritual, waiting to befall them. It's such an easy path to follow: from a distant look and acknowledgment of an attractive appearance; to open, flirtatious conversations; to private, serious heart-to-heart talks that involve the emotions; to physical involvement.

The Bible gives us warning signs all along the way: admonitions about chaste appearance, warnings about idle and flirtatious chatter, commands to communicate our emotional needs only to the spouse of our youth, advice to flee from sexual sin.

The principal reason for interest in sex outside marriage is the loss of a higher faith and purpose. To flee the emptiness in life, an individual looks for physical pleasure and emotional excitement. And those, the media tell us, are found in the excitement of illicit emotional involvement and sex.

For those who would argue, "Ours is not a casual thing. We care deeply for each other," the biblical warning is still the same. Eventually the guilt, the abandonment of God's blessing, and our shattered testimony destroy us.

"But I'm like David, who was involved with Bathsheba," say others. "I still love the Lord, even though I've given in to temptation." The primary fallacy with that claim and analogy is that they overlook repentance. King David's acknowledgment of sin did not stop with remorse and depression. He followed through with repentance, which can be defined only as obedience. He made things right.

Yes, God may know our heart, but our heart's condition is revealed in our conduct, and our conduct is 95 percent of our testimony to others on the job. As La Rochefoucauld reminds us, "It is much easier to suppress a first desire than to satisfy those that follow."

For Further Reflection:

Flee fornication. Every sin that a man doeth is without the body; but he that committeth fornication sinneth against his own body.

1 Corinthians 6:18

There hath no temptation taken you but such as is common to man: but God is faithful, who will not suffer you to be tempted above that ye are able; but will with the temptation also make a way to escape, that ye may be able to bear it.

1 Corinthians 10:13

For God wants you to be holy and pure, and to keep clear of all sexual sin so that each of you will marry in holiness and honor—not in lustful passion as the heathen do, in their ignorance of God and his ways.

And this also is God's will: that you never cheat in this matter by taking another man's wife, because the Lord will punish you terribly for this, as we have solemnly told you before. For God has not called us to be dirty-minded and full of lust, but to be holy and clean. If anyone refuses to live by these rules he is not disobeying the rules of men but of God who gives his Holy Spirit to you.

1 Thessalonians 4:3–8 TLB

21. Letting the Lips Fall Where They May

Be not hasty in thy spirit to be angry: for anger resteth in the bosom of fools.

Ecclesiastes 7:9

Self-control means controlling the tongue! A quick retort can ruin everything.

Proverbs 13:3 TLB

Let all bitterness, and wrath, and anger, and clamour, and evil speaking, be put away from you, with all malice.

Ephesians 4:31

A wise man controls his temper. He knows that anger causes mistakes.

Proverbs 14:29 TLB

Will Rogers once observed, "People who fly into a rage always make a bad landing." Anger on the job causes mistakes, leads people to jump to the wrong conclusions, saps productive energy and morale, creates untold conflict between employees and departments, and destroys a Christian witness.

"Well, that's just the way I am and just the way we run things. If you can't accept that, that's your problem." This sentiment is one we hear quite often from people who have something about them that others find offensive—especially when they don't want to accept responsibility for changing. Some people speak of a bad temper as if it were a curse they have to learn to live with, much like being born left-handed or having size-ten feet.

Not so. If control weren't a reasonable possibility, would God tell us to control our anger? The only kind of anger we're permitted is anger against sin. (When was the last time you saw anyone "pitch a fit" about someone's sin?)

Yet we hold onto our "right" to get angry about lesser matters. In fact, a hot temper is a useful tool for many individuals on the job. Others feed angry colleagues whatever they want, much like they feed roaring lions at the zoo. Secretaries quickly interrupt themselves to find their angry boss's missing management reports. Subordinates nod agreement to their belligerent manager's schedule, knowing they can't meet the promised deadlines. Service reps quickly return a call to the yelling customer who insulted the receptionist.

In addition to being a tool used to make others jump at our command, anger often is used to cover up for a lack of intelligence or poor performance. When someone in a meeting pounces on our inadequate investigation of a problem or on our weak conclusions, we often react with anger as a defense. The more put out we act with their "unreasonableness," the bigger cover we hope to spread over our head. When someone is wrong and can't admit it, he gets angry; when he's right, it is incredible how calm he can be.

The Bible speaks of several expressions of anger: cursing; jumping to the worst conclusion about people; complaining;

giving smart-aleck retorts; and being argumentative, over-sensitive, and bitter. These symptoms we don't need a check-list to uncover; they are usually readily apparent to all those around.

So how do we eliminate those overt signs of anger in our own conduct and attitude? Admit your anger, talk the problem through with those involved, and then ask God to remove it from your mind.

We *don't* get rid of anger by trying to bury it inside. The English poet William Blake penned this truth:

> *I was angry with my friend;*
> *I told my wrath, my wrath did end.*
> *I was angry with my foe;*
> *I told it not, my wrath did grow.*

An old Chinese proverb further warns: "The fire you kindle for your enemy often burns yourself more than him." Anger that we talk through in a calm way usually leads to forgiveness, reconciliation, and strength. The anger that we try to ignore or bury most often hardens into bitterness and a desire for revenge.

A bad temper distorts our perceptions and business judgments and makes us appear immature, undisciplined, and lacking in reason. An angry man makes those colleagues and customers who observe his outbursts his superiors.

For Further Reflection:

But I say unto you, That whosoever is angry with his brother without a cause shall be in danger of the judgment. . . .

Matthew 5:22

A fool is quick-tempered; a wise man stays cool when insulted.

Proverbs 12:16 TLB

Letting the Lips Fall Where They May

He that is soon angry dealeth foolishly: and a man of wicked devices is hated.

Proverbs 14:17

The discretion of a man deferreth his anger; and it is his glory to pass over a transgression.

Proverbs 19:11

But now ye also put off all these; anger, wrath, malice, blasphemy, filthy communication out of your mouth.

Colossians 3:8

22. Appraising on Performance or Appearance

Withhold not good from them to whom it is due, when it is in the power of thine hand to do it.

Proverbs 3:27

Don't be concerned about the outward beauty that depends on jewelry, or beautiful clothes, or hair arrangement. Be beautiful inside, in your hearts, with the lasting charm of a gentle and quiet spirit which is so precious to God.

1 Peter 3:3, 4 TLB

For as he thinketh in his heart, so is he. . . .

Proverbs 23:7

Researchers tell us that attractive people have an edge with first impressions. They are often thought to be brighter, smarter, more capable, and more personable than their un-attractive colleagues. Since these research findings were first published, the media have continued to bombard us with how-to's on making that all-important impression on the boss or the client.

The dress-for-success people tell us what color, what fabric, and what style suits to wear. Public relations firms emphasize the value of an appropriate company name, charging $35,000 to $50,000 to rename us and give us a fresh start. Management consultants remind us to circulate semiannual memos to our boss and colleagues that highlight our accomplishments on the job. Even politicians have joined the appearance-is-everything bandwagon, being coached on proper gestures and makeup for television appearances. Historians observe that for want of a good makeup man, Richard Nixon lost the 1960 election during his four debates with Kennedy.

Even outward behavior suggestive of underlying motives can be deceiving. You will recall the Acts 5 story of early Church members Ananias and Sapphira, who generously sold some of their property and donated the proceeds to the Church. Theirs was a good deed—almost. The problem was that they wanted their friends to think they were more generous than they really were. They reported to the Church a selling price far lower than what they actually received and pocketed the difference. The Holy Spirit struck them dead for their deception.

Behavior, although usually more revealing than appearance, may still present inaccuracies about one's true colors. With our limited discernment of others' motives, we can be fooled by the good done by someone with wrong motives; we can be equally deceived when harm is done by someone possessing the right motives and proper skills.

Nevertheless, supervisors must judge the outward performance of those they supervise, and colleagues often pass along opinions about their peers. Whether those judgments come formally in written performance appraisals or informally through oral praise or criticism, we should be careful to consider the whole person and the whole performance.

Personnel directors who specialize in training managers to conduct performance appraisals and review those appraisals often observe and warn against the "halo" and "pitchfork" tendencies. A supervisor who thinks someone is likable tends to rate that individual high in all performance areas. If the supervisor does not particularly like the employee or finds one or two objectionable traits or skill weaknesses, she tends to downgrade the employee in all areas.

Not only do inaccurate labels about weak performance do serious wrong; we often err with the mediocre to good labels. We cheat employees and ourselves by not recognizing the potential in those who consistently perform well without advertising themselves through the trappings of appearance.

Several years ago I had occasion to work with a large industrial and educational film producer on a video series and its accompanying workbooks. In all my years of writing, I have never worked with a more capable, conscientious editor than the one on that project. Clearly knowledgeable on every grammatical matter we discussed, he did not have to ask the whys and wherefores of editorial changes. Every suggestion and correction was made willingly and scrupulously. An outsider would have thought his name was going on the screen and book cover.

After concluding the project, I commented on the editor's expertise to a vice-president of the company, who responded: "Wayne? You don't say! Well, he's such a quiet guy. Minds his own business. I didn't know he was that kind of an employee. Maybe we should consider his capabilities for some other projects we're into."

Why not, indeed? Supervisors may get so caught up in the appearance-is-everything mode that they overlook their best workers.

We should continually monitor our own reaction to others:

- Do we selfishly hold our good employees back from deserved promotions simply because we don't want to lose them and don't want the hassle of training others to replace them?
- Do we let our own personality likes and dislikes color our judgments about work performance?
- Do we use our appraisals as opportunities to praise a job well done, as well as to point out areas of needed improvement?
- Do we suggest and provide further training, experience, or education for the future benefit of the employee?

As a man thinketh in his heart, so he is. That verse applies equally to the supervised and the supervisor.

For Further Reflection:

Be not a witness against your neighbor without cause, and do not deceive with your lips. Do not say, "I will do to him as he has done to me; I will pay the man back for what he has done."

Proverbs 24:28, 29 RSV

Let no evil talk come out of your mouths, but only such as is good for edifying, as fits the occasion, that it may impart grace to those who hear.

Ephesians 4:29 RSV

23. Boredom: The Boardroom Blues

The backslider gets bored with himself; the godly man's life is exciting.

Proverbs 14:14 TLB

But I say unto you, That every idle word that men shall speak, they shall give account thereof in the day of judgment.

Matthew 12:36

Many people consider boredom a mark of sophistication. They think it's plebeian to show wonder at or enthusiasm for almost any idea, event, or hopeful prospect. In fact, many of our movie idols and great writers have adopted cynicism as their worldview and gain satisfaction when media reviewers of their work comment on their perceptiveness about the human condition. You may have noticed the same pretense of cynicism or "sophistication" in colleagues who never laugh at anyone else's witticisms and never join in anyone else's excitement. In other words, they pride themselves on "not getting too excited" about anything in life.

Murmuring and griping, in addition to a pretense of sophistication, are other causes of boredom. "The habit of thinking ill of everything and everyone is tiresome to ourselves and to all around us," Pope John XXIII once remarked. A constant disposition of irritability and complaining makes any circumstances unhappy and meaningless for us.

However, a complaining disposition or attempts at sophistication are not the primary causes of boredom for the majority of us. The matter is much simpler or, depending on your perspective, more complex.

"A yawn may be defined as a silent yell," observes essayist and critic Gilbert Keith Chesterton. That yell may be one of anger and protest that life hasn't dealt with us properly. Or, it may be a scream that we ourselves don't even hear— a cry from the shallowness of our lives for something more meaningful to which to devote our days.

In fact, we become bored in direct proportion to our loss of interest in people and pursuits higher than ourselves. The biggest booster of boredom is selfishness. The more we indulge ourselves, the more we demand. Therefore, the more selfish we are, the more bored we get. Show me a person who dines every night on his favorite foods, who lives in a dream house, who can write a check for anything he wants, who has the ability to perform any necessary job skill, who calls any man his friend, and who is recognized by everybody in the marketplace, and I'll show you a very bored individual.

Bebe Moore Campbell, writing in *Savvy* magazine (September 1986), describes her own descent from commitment to burnout and boredom. She still vividly remembers the woman standing in front of her church pleading for volunteers to "pattern" her retarded child. Bebe persuaded three fourteen-year-old friends to join her each day in moving the limbs of this retarded child in the hope of helping her learn to crawl someday.

In college, she tutored a young boy with poor reading skills. She passed out petitions and marched to end the war in Vietnam. She met for endless hours to organize others and pressure school administrators into admitting more black students and hiring black faculty.

As a young adult, she wrote letters to prisoners and became a "big sister" for two children.

Bebe recites her earlier commitments to underscore who she has now become. Her commitment is no longer to hands-on help. Now, if she does anything at all, she merely writes a letter or sends a check. She has become lulled by self-centeredness, complacency, and abundance. The original flower child now dresses for success and has it her way at Burger King.

How about you? Do you ever look out the car window and see the street people scrounging for food? See the spaced-out teen wandering around the mall? See the unmarried pregnant teen with a cynical sneer and a cigarette hanging from her lip? Hear the neighbor drive the car through the garage wall and then shout at his family for nagging him about drunk driving? Observe the lonely eyes of the divorced mother alone at Christmastime without her children? See a college student shuffling across the parking lot with no place to go during the holidays? Read Position Wanted ads in the newspapers? Remember the elderly aunt in the nursing home?

Sitting dog-tired on the subway or in your car during rush-hour traffic after another long, boring day, do you ever look around you and think *Somebody ought to do something* about all those needs?

Only a mission higher than ourselves can extinguish boredom and ignite excitement in our lives. As near as your phone, there's an agency, an organization, or a church waiting for your call.

Boredom: The Boardroom Blues

For Further Reflection:

And whatsoever ye do, do it heartily, as to the Lord, and
not unto men.

Colossians 3:23

24. Corporate Compassion

When you help the poor you are lending to the Lord—and he pays wonderful interest on your loan!

Proverbs 19:17 TLB

Thus speaketh the Lord of hosts, saying, Execute true judgment, and shew mercy and compassions every man to his brother.

Zechariah 7:9

But when you do a kindness to someone, do it secretly—don't tell your left hand what your right hand is doing. And your Father who knows all secrets will reward you.

Matthew 6:3, 4 TLB

A recent newspaper headline read: SHUT DOWN "MIS-MANAGED" MS CHARITY, REPORT URGES. The story went on to focus on mismanagement and excessive staff salaries for the

ARMS charity, a self-help group for multiple sclerosis victims. Unfortunately, such stories are not rare, and many corporations and individuals use them as excuses to turn an unconcerned glance toward the needy and then go back to the computer: Business as usual.

Another line of reasoning that helps some businesspeople turn a cold shoulder to need is the "pull one's self up by the bootstraps" philosophy. Former HEW Secretary John W. Gardner refuses to brush the poverty problem away so easily: "For every talent poverty has stimulated, it has blighted a hundred" (*Newsweek,* June 2, 1986).

For every businessperson who claims that most of every dollar spent on charity and compassion is wasted, there are thousands who disagree. We've all heard of the Ronald McDonald Houses that shelter families of hospitalized children receiving extended medical treatment. In fact, the Ronald McDonald's Children's Charities, set up in Ray Kroc's memory after his 1984 death, have also contributed $2 million to other groups helping children.

Other philanthropic efforts by organizations such as the Gannett Foundation and B. Dalton Bookseller have been undertaken to help those seventeen to twenty-one million illiterate adults who can't read the front page of a newspaper, the warning on a can of poison, or a sign that says, IN CASE OF EMERGENCY, PUSH THIS BUTTON.

Corporate Angel Network (CAN) was the compassionate idea of a former cancer patient and licensed pilot, Priscilla Blum. She had noticed that numerous corporate airplanes flew in and out of the airport every day with empty seats. Why not see if they would fly cancer patients free to their distant medical treatments whenever they made routine business flights? The idea was not without problems because corporate flight schedules are sporadic and often canceled.

Guideposts magazine tells the story of how, upon such a cancellation, the Norton Simon company chairman phoned CAN to apologize and ask what he could do personally to help these victims. A staff member suggested he write a letter to his colleagues in other corporations and ask for their help. As a result, one hundred corporations signed up to transport patients through this nonprofit organization in White Plains, New York.

The list is almost endless for corporations that want to reach out to those in need:

- *Medical programs:* Red Cross blood bank drives, medical research projects, CPR training, and wellness campaigns.
- *Educational assistance:* Summer work programs, scholarships, speakers, equipment donations to local schools.
- *Fund-raising drives:* Donations and publicity to encourage support of local charities.
- *Counseling programs:* Help for alcohol and drug abusers, marital and family problems, financial and retirement planning.

But, you may be thinking, corporations can *afford* to have compassion for the problems of the world. They do it for publicity, for tax deductions, or even for profit. Before you write off all such efforts to motives of self-interest, consider the *individuals* who often initiate or become involved in such projects.

Carla Weaver, profiled in a recent *Houston Chronicle* story, held a corporate planning manager's job with Pennzoil and dreamed of feeding the poor with nutritious, inexpensive soybean meals. Carla wrote and got approved a corporate policy that granted a leave of absence for employees involved in charitable activities.

Then she left her fast-track job and went to Costa Rica, dipped into her savings to set up a small factory with four employees, and ordered 17,000 pounds of soybeans and several tons of rice and macaroni. She has sold the nutritious, inexpensive, easy-to-prepare food to the public school systems and many companies with employee cafeterias and hopes to market it to other underdeveloped countries in Central America and around the world. Although any such business has to be profitable to operate, her drive was compassion as she followed a Costa Rican friend and minister around the country.

Then there's Carl Umland, retired from Exxon Chemicals. He joined the Christian organization Habitat for Humanity to construct new homes to sell at cost, financed by interest-free loans for the poor. The houses are built primarily by volunteer labor with donated supplies. All the money received goes into building more houses. Those who purchase the houses must volunteer 500 hours of labor, either to build their own homes or someone else's. Habitat for Humanity has built or refurbished more than 240 homes in the United States and over 600 homes in 18 foreign countries. This volunteer labor is their practical expression of their faith and God's command about helping "the least of these" (*Houston Chronicle*, February 2, 1987).

Another such person is Eugene Lang, a self-made millionaire, who changed the destiny of a sixth-grade class in East Harlem. Invited to speak at a sixth-grade graduation ceremony, Lang made this promise: "Stay in school, and I'll help pay the college tuitions for each and every one of you!" And both sides have kept their promise. Six years later, the trust fund has grown to $250,000, and Lang says that more funds are available if needed. Even if he dies, his will guarantees payment of the college tuitions. A school administrator reports that 90 percent of that sixth-grade class has stayed in school. Following Lang's example, six other philanthropists have adopted classes in New York City (*Parade Magazine*, September 7, 1986).

And finally, before you pass off a lack of compassion because of waste, fraud, or your own lack of funds, consider other ways that a compassionate heart contributes to the world. Thoughtfulness, sensitivity, and kindness are often worth much more than money. In fact, when we compare good and evil in the world, much of the difference between the two can be labeled compassion.

Although we have little hesitation in categorizing as evil

the acts of a murderer, a rapist, a terrorist, or a drug dealer, we often fail to see the lack of compassion in the everyday acts or nonacts around us.

A lack of compassion may simply mean looking "through" a co-worker in need of attention. Have you ever noticed how your colleagues lay aside paper and pen, clutch pocketbooks, and putter toward the elevators at lunchtime leaving one person unnoticed and uninvited? Or how, in a meeting, when ideas are forthcoming and "massaged" with yeas and nays, one timidly offered idea fetches not a word, a glance, or a second thought and serves its giver as a reminder of the isolation enforced by an insensitive group?

Again and again, the New Testament tells us that Jesus looked at the multitudes with compassion. But it often cost Him time, effort, and popularity. Are we willing, as corporations or individuals, to do the same?

Never will we be more Christlike than in our moments of compassion.

For Further Reflection:

He that despiseth his neighbour sinneth: but he that hath mercy on the poor, happy is he.

Proverbs 14:21

Finally, be ye all of one mind, having compassion one of another, love as brethren, be pitiful, be courteous.

1 Peter 3:8

25. Conflict With Co-workers: The Paul and Barnabas Battle

If it be possible, as much as lieth in you, live peaceably with all men. Dearly beloved, avenge not yourselves, but rather give place unto wrath: for it is written, Vengeance is mine; I will repay, saith the Lord.

Romans 12:18, 19

Do all things without murmurings and disputings: That ye may be blameless and harmless, the sons of God, without rebuke, in the midst of a crooked and perverse nation, among whom ye shine as lights in the world.

Philippians 2:14, 15

One of the most frustrating experiences in human relationships is when we learn another person doesn't share our viewpoints, expectations, needs, or values. Perhaps we take a look at the long-range problems, and others see only the short-term benefits. Maybe we thrive on risk, and others value security. We may push thoroughness, and others may preach speed.

You'll note that the Apostle Paul didn't admonish us never to express our differences. Instead, he says, "If at all possible" live in peace with all men. We can work out or give in to conflicts over schedules, wants, needs, or goals. Only those conflicts of value are unavoidable.

A few years back a friend of mine had no choice but to resign his job over one such value conflict. As manager of a major discount store, he was put in the awkward position of having to deal with the nationwide chain's fraudulent practice against various manufacturers who advertised through discount coupons. The practice was for the store personnel to take off all the discount coupons attached to the merchandise, which were meant for the consumer, and mail them back to the manufacturer for the rebates.

Senior management of the discount chain justified its action by explaining that the consumer wasn't hurt in any way. The store simply reduced the price of the item by the amount of the discount and passed on the savings. The result was that this chain could always advertise the lowest prices and undersell the competition. My manager friend had a conflict of values with senior management over this practice and had to quit his job.

But conflicts of wants, needs, and expectations *can* be resolved and deserve our best efforts.

Furthermore, conflict isn't something we should necessarily be ashamed of, because conflict can lead to better decisions and problem solving. Such was the case with the conflict between the Greeks and the Hebrews over the daily distribution of food to the widows among them (*see* Acts 6). As a result of the conflict's being brought out in the open and discussed, they selected seven deacons to carry on the daily administrative work of the Church.

Conflict can also be a benefit when it stretches us intellectually and emotionally. When someone challenges our ideas or actions, we have to review and reevaluate them to be able to defend them. If we discover that we can't defend them, then we're better off to discard them. Peter decided that was the case when confronted about the Gospel being for the Gentiles as well as for the Jews (Acts 10).

So how do we go about making conflict positive rather than negative on the job?

To begin with, as soon as we roll up our sleeves to resolve a conflict, we should try to wash our ego from our work. Have you ever noticed how we make introductions? "This is Harriet Hargrove, an accountant who works with our revenue section." Or, "This is Bill Bright, the engineer who designed this year's model virtually single-handedly." At work, we're known for our work. Therefore, when someone points out a disagreement or change or error, we often feel as though they are attacking us personally.

If we could only drain the ego from ourselves in much the same way that a mechanic lets the air out of a tire before repairing it, we probably wouldn't find disagreement so disagreeable.

With ego out of the way, we're ready to talk things over. Self-control is rarely more difficult than when discussing a disagreement. "A man without self-control is as defenseless as a city with broken-down walls" (Proverbs 25:28 TLB). We can't possibly come up with a long-lasting, effective resolution until we have ourselves under control— much less have the conflict under control.

With self-control, it's much easier to treat the other person with respect and basic good manners, both musts if we intend to make the resolution a lasting one. Manners are what separate the civilized from the barbarians. Manners restrain one's self, give preference to others, create order out of chaos, collect the educated and the uneducated into one profile, and march them toward the same goal. I would dare to say that more conflicts in the corporate world result from a simple lack of manners than from genuine needs or values.

In all conflict resolution, we must also be very careful not to wound another's self-esteem. "Well, if you had returned my phone call yesterday before we went into that meeting, rather than bumbling around in your usual daydream world. . . ." Needless to say, this type of response does not induce people to return phone calls more promptly in the future. We should never attack the person but rather discuss only the action or behavior that needs changing.

Finally, as we get around to stating our views and hearing those of our co-worker, there's one last consideration. According to English essayist Joseph Addison: "If men would consider not so much wherein they differ, as wherein they agree, there would be far less of uncharitableness and angry feeling in the world."

Find areas of agreement before you launch into the deep of disagreement. Do you have the same profit goals? Do you both want to please the customer? Where do your facts, opinions, or goals match? That's the starting point for resolving differences.

If, after long discussion, you don't see your divergent positions coming together, remember that some differences may not need to be resolved. Both sides may be right, as early New Testament missionaries Paul and Barnabas discovered. Their conflict over whether to take young John Mark along with them eventually led to their pursuing the same goals (Acts 15). Although John Mark hadn't been exactly what they'd needed on their first missionary journey, Barnabas believed in giving him a second chance. People need second chances; Barnabas was right.

But so was Paul. Perhaps he felt that time to spread the Gospel was short, that they didn't have time to waste on encouraging or training the younger, less-committed workers. Paul and his future circumstances—prison, stonings, beatings—demanded nothing less than total commitment.

Two sides can be right. Paul and Barnabas accepted that, and each went his own way.

Supreme Court Justice William O. Douglas observed: "Today it is generally recognized that all corporations possess an element of public interest. A corporation director must think not only of the stockholder but also of the laborer, the supplier, the purchaser, and the ultimate consumer. Our economy is but a chain which can be no stronger than any one of its links. We all stand together or fall together in our highly industrialized society of today."

If we can keep this fragility in our minds as we discuss our work conflicts, resolutions might more often and more quickly tap us on the shoulder.

For Further Reflection:

A brother offended is harder to be won than a strong city: and their contentions are like the bars of a castle.

Proverbs 18:19

He who meddles in a quarrel not his own is like one who takes a passing dog by the ears.

Proverbs 26:17 RSV

Let all bitterness, and wrath, and anger, and clamour, and evil speaking, be put away from you, with all malice.

Ephesians 4:31

And unto him that smiteth thee on the one cheek offer also the other; and him that taketh away thy cloke forbid not to take thy coat also.

Luke 6:29

26. Cooperation: The Mary and Martha Dilemma

And if any man will sue thee at the law, and take away thy coat, let him have thy cloke also. And whosoever shall compel thee to go a mile, go with him twain. Give to him that asketh thee, and from him that would borrow of thee turn not thou away.

Matthew 5:40–42

But Martha was cumbered about much serving, and came to him, and said, Lord, dost thou not care that my sister hath left me to serve alone? bid her therefore that she help me.

Luke 10:40

I receive a call from the education coordinator at a client's office, who is trying to ready things for our next seminar. Could we immediately ship her twenty-four books for the attendees? Someone from the purchasing department, she assures us, will get in touch in a few days to give us the billing information. Sure. We send the books.

A few weeks later, we phone the responsible person in the purchasing department to ask about the paperwork. She has no paperwork, knows nothing about the order, and does not have time to check on it for us. Okay. So we just wait.

Two days later, a second person in the purchasing department phones to order twenty-four books. We explain that the twenty-four books have already been sent. He insists that he doesn't know anything about the first twenty-four books but that his paperwork says for him to order twenty-four books. We mention the *high* probability that this is the same order we have already shipped. Can he please check that out? No, that's "not his department." We give in and accept the second order, shipping another twenty-four books and billing with the purchase order number he gives.

Three days later, the person calls back and says he has too many books. He accepts no blame, saying that the person who told us to ship the books in the first place "was out of line." Will we accept the returned books? Yes.

An hour later, we get a call from the education coordinator in another branch about another seminar. Will we send twenty books? We explain that the purchasing department has just called, asking permission to return twenty-four books, and we suggest that they shuffle those books down the hall to her, rather than go to the trouble and expense and delay of returning them to us. Sure, she says, no problem.

The next day we get a call from the purchasing department, asking why we were billing for two shipments of twenty-four books. We give her all the details, including the names and phone numbers of her colleagues, and ask her to work out the problem. No, she insists, the education coordinators have no business phoning us themselves. No, she will not contact them to straighten out the mess. "Let them take care of it themselves."

I phone the education coordinator to verify that I should indeed send the extra books and not depend on the switch.

How dare the purchasing department, she grumbles, mess things up! Would she take the other names and phone numbers from me so she can straighten out the problem? No, she says. It's the purchasing department's fault; let them contact her.

The next day . . . well, I won't bore you with the rest of the logjam. You can probably think of several similar incidents of your own. In fact, some people seem to think that such mixups are inevitable in large bureaucracies. Maybe they are. But you, on the other hand, can do your best to avoid them where your job and department are concerned.

What causes an uncooperative attitude? Stubbornness. Pride. Laziness. Jealousies—comparing your paycheck or workload or abilities to someone else's. Perhaps resentment, a sense of someone's not pulling his or her own weight, and the feeling of frustration at having to "pick up the slack."

Such was the case between Mary and Martha during Jesus' visit. Mary had chosen the better part of sitting at Jesus' feet. Martha permitted herself to feel like a martyr and to become resentful of the added responsibilities of a guest meal when Mary felt no such responsibility and offered no help.

Some employers and bosses purposely set up competitive situations that breed resentment and jealousy rather than cooperation. Harvard professor, author, and management consultant Dr. Rosabeth Moss Kanter has dubbed these competitive environments "cowboy management."

Cowboy management makes competition, rather than cooperation, a virtue. Cowboy managers like to get out there in the wilderness with a few trusty pals and no company or government restraints. They practice survival of the fittest for their product, service, idea, or department. Kanter has conducted extensive research to see if this kind of competition has been successful in the major corporations across the nation.

Success with this philosophy was rare. Kanter found that creating winners and losers within the corporation was bad strategy. In well-managed, successful organizations, the competition was a race against the clock or the task, not against other employees. In other words, in a successful sales campaign, reps battled to surpass their own past sales volumes or to achieve a certain percentage increase in territories that did not overlap their colleagues'.

In Kanter's words: "In every high-performing company I've seen—in my own research and consulting practice as well as in that of other researchers—cooperation was more effective than competition in fostering productivity and innovation" (*Savvy*, October 1986, p. 36).

Another recent study shows similar results in day-to-day management decisions. Dr. John P. Kotter of the Harvard Business School observed the daily activities of fifteen successful top managers to discover their management style. He concluded that although senior managers occasionally exercised authority by issuing directives, they generally used subtle means of persuasion and tried to gain others' cooperation rather than demanding that they blindly follow orders against their will (*Small Business Report*, February 1987).

Management consultants and professors merely confirm what the Bible has told us all along about the human spirit: We cannot sincerely help other people without helping ourselves in the process. We gain spiritual benefit and nourishment from a cooperative, not a competitive, attitude.

Going the second mile is a testimony to our non-Christian colleagues. Our serving when we'd rather be sitting may be just what a colleague needs to refresh his or her spirit on the job. In doing so with the right attitude, we may in turn refresh our own spirits.

It's simply a value-added consideration that our corporations, as well as our people, run more successfully on cooperation than competition.

For Further Reflection:

With all lowliness and meekness, with longsuffering, forbearing one another in love; Endeavouring to keep the unity of the Spirit in the bond of peace.

Ephesians 4:2, 3

27. Corporate Courtesy

And as ye would that men should do to you, do ye also to them likewise.

Luke 6:31

Love is very patient and kind, never jealous or envious, never boastful or proud, never haughty or selfish or rude. Love does not demand its own way. It is not irritable or touchy. It does not hold grudges and will hardly even notice when others do it wrong.

1 Corinthians 13:4, 5 TLB

There's something about walking into a business office that makes otherwise courteous people shed their social mores and become barbarians. Why else would we have to put signs in the rest room that say, PLEASE DEPOSIT TOWELS IN THE WASTEBASKET and signs above the water fountain that say, FOR SANITARY PURPOSES, PLEASE DO NOT SPIT IN THIS FOUNTAIN? Is boorish behavior contagious?

Standing in line at a copier at the public library, I observed this incident. A woman making copies from a pile of journal articles noticed a man waiting impatiently behind her. She turned to him and explained that since she had so much copying to do, she would stop for a moment and permit him to make his copy. He nodded, not too gratefully, and she stepped aside, whereupon the man literally took over the machine for multiple copies, keeping her waiting for quite some time to finish the chore she had so graciously interrupted for him.

For the traveling businessperson, rudeness is rampant on the road: in taxis, planes, restaurants, and hotels. At Washington's Dulles Airport, I crawled into a taxi about midnight. When I gave the taxi driver the name of a nearby hotel, he began to curse me and his bad luck for getting all the short fares. For the entire four-minute ride, he cursed the whole United States government and economic system for exploiting foreigners.

The everyday insensitivities around all of us are endless: not returning phone calls, leaving spilled coffee on the snack-room chair, keeping other meeting attendees waiting while you do "just one more thing," looking through people who smile and speak in the halls.

Some people plead ignorance about such rudeness. A trainer at a major corporation asked to keep a software package we had demonstrated, so she could show it to others who had input into the buying decision. A week later, a sales rep called her, wanting to pick up the demo package to show another client; he left a complete message about the nature of his call.

When she did not return the call, he tried again. First, the trainer was "unavailable"; then she was "in a training session"; then she was "in a meeting"; then she was "out of the office for a few days." Five months later, the sales rep gave up trying to get her on the phone and wrote a letter explaining that he needed the demo package returned.

By overnight express, the sales rep got the package and an

apology letter from the trainer saying she was so sorry. She had forgotten she still had the package and would have returned the phone calls if she'd known that was why he was calling.

Wasn't the sales rep due an apology for the unreturned calls, regardless of his reason for calling?

Why do these discourtesies happen? Some see customers, callers, and colleagues as all alike—faceless people in a crowded sea of corporate competition. Our high-tech marketplace has fostered low-touch relationships.

But the fact that other people are insensitive or rude to us should not dictate our own response. Someone has said that a test of good manners is being able to put up pleasantly with bad ones. Good manners may require a little sacrifice on our part: a little time, a little forethought, extra steps out of our way, extra strokes of the pen or keyboard.

"Life is not so short but that there is always time for courtesy," insisted Ralph Waldo Emerson. Even as Christ hurried through the crowds on a busy day, He stopped when one believing woman touched the hem of His garment. He wasn't too busy to acknowledge her, even commenting on her faith and insight in coming to Him. No doubt Jesus delegated some of His ministry to His twelve assistants, but we have the same option. We, too, can have an assistant take or give a message or return a call or a kindness.

Courtesy is really a matter of sensitivity to others' needs and feelings. Author Jonathan Swift wisely observed, "Good manners is the art of making those people easy with whom we converse. Whoever makes the fewest people uneasy is the best bred in the company."

Recently I attended an informational meeting where we had two speakers, the vice-president of the company and the controller. The meeting attendees were middle managers who'd flown in from across the country for a briefing on a new budgeting procedure. The controller made her presentation about the whys and wherefores of the new budgeting procedures, using the most complex jargon possible and illustrating authorizations for expenditures in the millions of dollars.

After she finished, the vice-president called her to the side and made the following suggestion: "Before the next group comes in, why don't you plan to tone down the illustrations a little? These people don't have the authority to approve the kind of dollars you're talking about. Let's use figures that are a little more in line with their responsibilities. We don't want them to feel unimportant in the scheme of things."

From watching this VP shake hands and visit with his managers around the room, I got the distinct impression that he had the same sensitivity to others in all his dealings. Maybe your experience has been much the same as mine and the anonymous people who keep saying, "The bigger they are, the nicer they are." Courtesy is sensitivity.

But common courtesy is not all that common in corporate America. In fact, it has almost become a contradiction in terms. Why shouldn't courtesy become a cause for the Christian?

For Further Reflection:

A soft answer turneth away wrath. . . .

Proverbs 15:1

Don't be selfish; don't live to make a good impression on others. Be humble, thinking of others as better than yourself. Don't just think about your own affairs, but be interested in others, too, and in what they are doing.

Philippians 2:3, 4 TLB

28. Paying Your Debts When the Debits Say You Can't

Don't withhold repayment of your debts. Don't say "some other time," if you can pay now.

Proverbs 3:27, 28 TLB

The rich ruleth over the poor, and the borrower is servant to the lender.

Proverbs 22:7

Can you imagine the size of the army the United States could field if the government used soon-to-be King David's recruiting method outlined in 1 Samuel 22:2? His soldiers were debtors; they had few choices open to them. With the typical American owing thousands of dollars, a good many debtors feel enough desperation to escape the burden by any means available—whether that means joining a foreign guerrilla army or faking an accident and beginning a new life under an assumed name.

Although most would agree that many people are living far beyond their means, many would also condemn themselves and these fellow undisciplined souls who have gotten themselves into such a predicament.

On the other hand, businesses often have a totally different perspective on the matter of paying their debts. They often rob Peter to pay Paul—or don't pay Paul at all.

Certainly if a business has a "net thirty days" agreement, it makes good business sense to keep the use of its money as long as possible. But what about those times when there's no such agreement, when businesses knowingly violate the trust of their creditors or even their employees?

A Houston manufacturing company employing over five hundred people recently blew the whistle at 5:00 P.M. Friday and then announced that it was filing for bankruptcy. None of the employees received their paychecks for the last two weeks' work, even though the company had decided to file for bankruptcy before the pay period began. In fact, they'd made an agreement with the bookkeeper that if she stayed on two extra weeks to wind things up, she'd get a paycheck and be the only employee not left holding the bag.

As married college students, my husband and I had similar difficulties with an employer. My husband worked for a roofer who frequently duped his employees out of their wages. They were told to collect the tags off the bundles of shingles as they put each bundle on the houses during the workweek. On the last workday of each week, they were supposed to turn in their tags and collect so many dollars per tag.

Quite frequently, the roofer refused to pay his employees (almost exclusively students working their way through college) the full amount he owed them, claiming that someone had stolen extra tags from other job sites and turned in too many. Therefore, he would summarily subtract a few tags, or forty to sixty dollars, from each worker's paycheck.

On many paydays, he failed to show up at quitting time, sending word that he was tied up and his employees would have to catch him later for their money. The truth was that his employees often had to drop by the office four or five times before catching him several days later and getting their paychecks.

Nowadays, one student in seven defaults on his federal education loan. Common practice? Yes. Ethical? No.

Does being in debt make good business sense? Businesses under heavy debt lose their freedom. They often make decisions not according to preference but under pressure. Debtors lack the freedom to experiment with new ideas that might be risky but promising for the future.

Some companies and individuals despair of ever being able to pay off their debt and consequently give up the challenge. "Poverty is hard, but debt is horrible," observed evangelist Charles Spurgeon.

Not only does debt restrict freedom, but it also leads to compromise. In Luke 16 we read about the servant who scurried around to those who owed his master money and offered them the "opportunity" to repay only half of their total debt. Debt often leads sensible, honest people into compromises they would never make under ordinary circumstances.

Finally, debt can be an expression of our lack of faith in God to adequately meet our needs. Elisha commanded the widow to sell her remaining oil, pay her debt, and be prepared to live on the rest (2 Kings 4:7). Some of us have refused to operate our businesses or live our lives on what God provides.

Debts destroy our testimony, usurp our freedom, cause us to compromise our convictions, and often make poor business sense. Think about it the next time you're tempted to say, "Charge it."

For Further Reflection:

The wicked borrows, and cannot pay back, but the righteous is generous and gives.

Psalms 37:21 RSV

The robbery of the wicked shall destroy them; because they refuse to do judgment.

Proverbs 21:7

Then she came and told the man of God. And he said, Go, sell the oil, and pay thy debt, and live thou and thy children of the rest.

2 Kings 4:7

29. Haman's Hang-ups About Enemies

Rejoice not when thine enemy falleth, and let not thine heart be glad when he stumbleth.

Proverbs 24:17

Never falsely accuse a man to his employer, lest he curse you for your sin.

Proverbs 30:10 TLB

Don't repay evil for evil. Wait for the Lord to handle the matter.

Proverbs 20:22 TLB

When a man's ways please the Lord, he maketh even his enemies to be at peace with him.

Proverbs 16:7

Will Rogers reportedly never met a man he didn't like, but he dared not speculate that all those he met liked him! All people who stand for certain values, causes, or ideas are bound to find those who oppose them. Even Jesus had enemies.

For most of us, it's not those enemies that plague us—those who dislike us because of our righteousness or the good we do. Instead, most of us create enemies unnecessarily. We make enemies because of our own stubbornness, lack of sensitivity, selfishness, unkindness, jealousy, or pride. Those are the enemies we need to learn to deal with in a positive way.

In the book of Esther, we see how Haman created his own enemy, Mordecai, because of pride and jealousy. When Jewish Mordecai refused to bow down to Haman as the king's official, Haman grew perturbed enough to talk the king into signing a decree saying that all those Jews who practiced such "strange" customs and had allegiances other than to the king should be put to death. As time went on, Haman's jealousy toward Mordecai grew.

First, the king ordered Haman to parade through the city streets, leading Mordecai dressed in the king's robe and riding the king's donkey as a reward for a long-forgotten good deed toward the king—a reward Haman thought he himself deserved. Twice Haman went home to complain to his wife about the favor the king showed to Mordecai rather than to himself.

Finally, determined to put a stop to his perceived enemy, Haman had a gallows built on which he planned to have Mordecai hanged. But before Haman could get rid of his enemy, Mordecai talked his niece, Queen Esther, into intervening with the king on behalf of the Jewish people and saving them from Haman's plot of death. Together they thwarted Haman's plans. The king was so outraged with Haman that he had him hanged on the gallows Haman had planned to use for his enemy, Mordecai.

If we learn anything from Haman's hanging, we learn how

not to treat the enemies we create. First, we learn that we can't ignore them. According to an Italian proverb: "Have you fifty friends? It is not enough. Have you one enemy? It is too much." An enemy ignored does no one any good. We need to learn to deal with our behavior and attitudes that create the enemy.

Gaining victory over an enemy should not be the goal. If we squelch our enemy for the moment, we have at best gained a little time for our own pursuits; we have not removed the cause or the ill will. Only when we reconcile the enemy—change his or her will or attitude toward us—can we say we have dealt positively with that person.

So how do we reconcile an enemy? First, we have to get rid of the impulse for revenge. Such was certainly not the case with Haman. When the king wanted to honor Mordecai for his earlier good deed in foiling an assassination plot, Haman certainly had the power to do good. The problem was that he hated being in that position! Unlike Haman, our own hearts have to be set for the cause of reconciliation rather than conflict.

The poet Longfellow once observed, "If we could read the secret history of our enemies, we should find in each man's life sorrow and suffering enough to disarm all hostility." Try to understand your enemy's viewpoint and motive, and with that understanding you will soften your own heart. The impulse to punish is powerful; only the love of God can drain that urge.

A second way Haman dealt with his self-created enemy was to cast doubt on him through half-truths. By alluding to the "strange" Jewish customs and their allegiance to God, Haman implied that the Jews would show disrespect to King Ahasuerus and do him harm.

It's still a favorite ploy of some people to use such half-truths to undo their enemies. In front of a group of co-workers, they ask questions like: "Have you finally completed the report that you had such difficulty understanding?" "Have you been able to stop so many of your good employees from wanting to transfer out of your department?" "Did you phone your senator opposing that bill, or do you favor taking advantage of the poor?"

In fact, questions of this nature on political subjects have been used to unfairly sabotage good men by forcing yes or no answers on complex issues. We would do well to avoid Haman's example of using half-truths to produce erroneous conclusions.

Another matter in dealing with enemies is learning to listen to them. That's right—listen to them. We should realize that our enemies may have a point about us. In fact, we may come much closer to the truth of our situation by examining our enemy's opinion of ourselves rather than our own.

Finally, we must do unto our enemies as if they were our friends, just as we would have them treat us. Haman all too clearly learned the wisdom of that truth when the gallows meant for Mordecai became the means of his own death.

Shakespeare penned his own version of this biblical truth in a rather specific analogy: "Heat not a furnace for your foe so hot that it do singe yourself." Many businesspeople, I'm sure, could make similar analogies from past experience:

- "Set not the sales quota so high for your despised salesperson that the CEO chides you, the manager, for not reaching it."
- "Assign not all the unpopular, gruesome projects to one disliked employee until she becomes discouraged and resigns, leaving you in a lurch."
- "Withhold not needed data from the report writer, or the vice-president will ask you to plan your next budget according to the report's erroneous information."

Taking care not to create enemies unnecessarily and reconciling those we have is often our strongest test of Christian maturity.

For Further Reflection:

If thine enemy be hungry, give him bread to eat; and if he be thirsty, give him water to drink: For thou shalt heap coals of fire upon his head, and the Lord shall reward thee.

Proverbs 25:21, 22

If it be possible, as much as lieth in you, live peaceably with all men. Dearly beloved, avenge not yourselves, but rather give place unto wrath: for it is written, Vengeance is mine; I will repay, saith the Lord.

Romans 12:18, 19

Ye have heard that it hath been said, An eye for an eye, and a tooth for a tooth: But I say unto you, That ye resist not evil: but whosoever shall smite thee on thy right cheek, turn to him the other also. And if any man will sue thee at the law, and take away thy coat, let him have thy cloke also. And whosoever shall compel thee to go a mile, go with him twain.

Matthew 5:38–41

30. A Stressed Conscience

But if ye do not forgive, neither will your Father which is in heaven forgive your trespasses.

Mark 11:26

Therefore if thou bring thy gift to the altar, and there rememberest that thy brother hath ought against thee; Leave there thy gift before the altar, and go thy way; first be reconciled to thy brother, and then come and offer thy gift.

Matthew 5:23, 24

A man's home is his castle, they say. Perhaps that's true for many people because home is the only place they can go to get out from under the pressure of a stressed conscience and escape the feeling country-western writers so colorfully phrase as "being done wrong."

When I recently asked an acquaintance how she liked her new job, she held her grim countenance and whispered conspiratorially, "Let's go to lunch sometime."

Later in the day, I had occasion to be in the department with her former colleagues, who happened to mention her transfer.

"She got a really good job, but she's never liked it. To keep from laying off people after the buyout and reorganization, management decided to shuffle us all around. And since Rebecca had just finished her MBA, they moved her to personnel. She could have been a real star there and just about set up the department any way she wanted it. But the thing was, she felt she had no choice. She couldn't understand why we all got to stay in this department and she was the only one to have to leave. She's never gotten over it. She's just miserable. We all used to get along so well; I just don't know why she thinks someone had it in for her."

According to Ephesians 4:31, the signs of a convicted conscience are anger, bitterness, and strife—whether we have been wronged or we have wronged others.

A church member recently shared with his congregation his conviction about a wrong done to his company. When he was transferred, he moved across the country with the understanding that his company would pay the moving expenses. But by the time he submitted all the expenses, the executive who'd made the promise had retired from the company. Result: The company would not reimburse him. The employee vowed to make the company regret that decision; he'd get even.

And he did. Over the next few years, he stole thousands of dollars worth of tools and spare parts from the company warehouse, rationalizing that the company "owed it to him." He even rationalized with the Lord, telling himself he had a "ministry" with the tools, because on weekends he repaired the cars of his family and friends without charge. One by one, these friends began to quit calling him for help. But again, he rationalized that this meant he could spend more time with his family.

Finally, conviction fell on him so strongly that he had to load up his garage full of tools, write out a check to cover all

154

the years' worth of spare parts, and confront his boss with the returned equipment and a confession.

The boss's response: "I don't think the company can afford to lose an employee who now has a clear conscience."

A clear conscience—both ours and the other person's—places demands on us, as employers and employees, in two ways. We must forgive, and we must be forgiven. A clear conscience is the ability to say we have made things right with every individual who has ever wronged us or whom we have ever wronged.

Excuses such as these do not let us off the hook: "But she was clearly in the wrong." "He doesn't even know about it." "It was such a minor issue."

For starters in gaining forgiveness and a clear conscience, try this on-the-job checklist:

- Have I ever padded a résumé?
- Have I ever gossiped about why someone left a job?
- Have I ever intentionally given the wrong impression about someone or some competitor's company by what I said or left unsaid?
- Have I ever taken credit for someone else's ideas or accomplishments, passing them off as my own?
- Have I ever pouted, complained, or wished evil for someone because of his promotion, bonus, or award?

Probably the biggest question is: "Have I ever refused to really forgive someone for hurting me in these same ways?" If so, rethink your position. The parable in Matthew 18 tells about the debtor who was forgiven a great debt when he pleaded for mercy, then had his fellowman thrown in prison for a paltry debt he couldn't repay.

By both asking and offering forgiveness, we rid ourselves of a stressed conscience. We gain emotional freedom, peace of mind, and God's forgiveness for our own errors as well. Begrudging forgiveness saps the joy out of an otherwise productive day. How can you lose by giving up a grudge?

For Further Reflection:

He that covereth his sins shall not prosper: but whoso confesseth and forsaketh them shall have mercy.

Proverbs 28:13

Forbearing one another, and forgiving one another, if any man have a quarrel against any: even as Christ forgave you, so also do ye. And above all these things put on charity, which is the bond of perfectness.

Colossians 3:13, 14

And forgive us our debts, as we forgive our debtors.

Matthew 6:12

31. Where Your Treasure Is: Stockholders and Sunday Morning Offerings

But this I say, He which soweth sparingly shall reap also sparingly; and he which soweth bountifully shall reap also bountifully. Every man according as he purposeth in his heart, so let him give; not grudgingly, or of necessity: for God loveth a cheerful giver.

2 Corinthians 9:6, 7

Lay not up for yourselves treasures upon earth, where moth and rust doth corrupt, and where thieves break through and steal: But lay up for yourselves treasures in heaven, where neither moth nor rust doth corrupt, and where thieves do not break through nor steal: For where your treasure is, there will your heart be also.

Matthew 6:19–21

Honour the Lord with thy substance, and with the firstfruits of all thine increase: So shall thy barns be filled with plenty, and thy presses shall burst out with new wine.

Proverbs 3:9, 10

What I gave, I have; what I spent, I had; what I kept, I lost. That old epitaph couldn't be more biblical and more appropriate for those of us in the business world.

The Bible has much to say about money. It doesn't refer just to what we give directly to God in our tithes and offerings, but also includes giving to advance His causes in the world while helping the needy along the way. The emphasis on money is well placed, because the way we handle the money we earn determines how much of it we keep—eternally.

Promises of prosperity almost always follow the principles of giving. No matter how much we give away, God promises that we will still have all our physical needs met, that our children will not go hungry, and that we will know true contentment. Those promises come in pint-size or giant-size.

Back when my husband was a seminary student, we struggled along on two part-time salaries and had few extras. One December we received eighty dollars in a Christmas card, with directions to buy gifts for our toddlers. But only hours before, I had spoken with a neighbor who had a much more pressing need than ours that Christmas. Her husband had deserted her and her four children, leaving them destitute, and her electricity was about to be shut off for nonpayment. One of the greatest pleasures I've ever had was tucking that money into another envelope and sliding it under the neighbor's door before the 4:00 deadline given by the utility company.

But that wasn't the end of the story. I would have been satisfied if it had been, for all the pleasure I'd received from knowing I'd met a real, desperate need in someone's life. In the week that followed, my husband and I got two more checks in the mail from loving church members—enough to buy Christmas presents, to pay our next semester's tuition, and even to have leftovers to put in the bank.

Although there have been many of God's repayments through the years, let me move to a recent giant-size one. My husband lost his job after we'd just pledged a large extra offering, above our regular tithe, to a church building program. Scared? Yes, we were. But since God had tutored us all through the years about His giving principles, we continued our weekly pledges for the many months my husband was without steady work. During that first year, my struggling business took off through no effort of my own, and our year's receipts were almost four times that of the previous year—abundantly more than enough to cover our extra pledge.

Stories such as these abound from those far wealthier and far more generous than I am. I wish I could say that my husband and I have always been so trusting and generous, but we haven't, and that's what has led me to study the next question: Why don't we *always* see prosperity immediately follow giving? Our problem may come with a defective attitude about the whole giving/prosperity cycle.

One such inappropriate attitude in giving is to think God can be bribed to provide success. As the biblical writer noted, we tend to consider giving to God only when we're staring at red ink on the balance sheet. "God, if You'll just . . . then I promise that I'll give. . . ." God isn't a broker, and He doesn't delight in such deals.

Another wrong attitude is giving to cover conscience. We pull some shady shenanigan to win a bid and clinch a deal, then try to salve our conscience by giving God half the profit. Or we feel a tug on our heart to share some time and attention with a down-in-the-mouth co-worker, but our time is so limited; why not just write a check and pay somebody else to do good?

God is not interested in weighing our gifts on a scale according to our deeds. The Pharisees were ever so careful to tithe every tidbit of income, and rightly so, but Jesus assured them that monetary gifts didn't cover all the other matters they left undone. Giving is no substitute for obedience.

Still another faulty attitude is a begrudging spirit, whether we're giving to God or to others. We often hear this question about gifts to the church: "How *much* should I give?" What these people are usually asking is, "How *little* can I give and still win God's favor?" With regard to how much, we should recall that the Pharisees' millions were not enough, but the widow's mite was more than enough.

Considering charity toward their fellowmen, some people begrudge giving so much that they hold onto all their money until the reading of their will. As someone once pointed out, the person who saves all his wealth until the time of his death only conveys to the world that he would have kept it to himself longer, if he could have! Giving only when death leaves us no better alternative may be pride's desire to leave a monument to one's self. Such a gift can even be motivated by fear; the dying person may hope the large sum will wipe out the debt of an unrighteous life.

Another wrong attitude is giving to buy friends. Some of those people close to the late rock singer Elvis Presley tell us that was his motivation for the impulsive giving of large gifts to total strangers. Cash for carry creates a multitude of charities at the marketplace door—some worthy, some not. As the proverb notes, givers have many "friends"; we have to have good sense in our giving, just as in every other decision.

So what is the right attitude about giving? Generosity and secrecy.

The English essayist Charles Lamb said, "The greatest pleasure I know is to do a good action by stealth, and to have it found out by accident." Have you ever wondered if the big bucks that corporations give to charity and then use as the basis of an advertising campaign will be deducted on God's account of blessings?

To pity the poor is human; to alleviate their need is generosity; to do so secretly is Godlike.

Finally, we should have a grateful attitude about our ability to give. A businessman once confided to his pastor that it hadn't been difficult to tithe when his check was only a hundred dollars a week. And it hadn't been too hard when he was making only a thousand a week. But, he lamented, with the kind of earnings he had at present, that 10 percent was an awfully big chunk. The pastor immediately knew how to solve his problem: "Then let's get on our knees and ask God if He can lower your salary back to what it was earlier."

Seneca observed: "This is the law of benefits between men; the one ought to forget at once what he has given, and the other ought never to forget what he has received."

Gratitude, not gain, is the proper motive for giving. We enjoy most those treasures and pleasures that we give away.

For Further Reflection:

Bring ye all the tithes into the storehouse, that there may be meat in mine house, and prove me now herewith, saith the Lord of hosts, if I will not open you the windows of heaven, and pour you out a blessing, that there shall not be room enough to receive it.

Malachi 3:10

It is well with the man who deals generously and lends, who conducts his affairs with justice. For the righteous will never be moved; he will be remembered for ever. He is not afraid of evil tidings; his heart is firm, trusting in the Lord. His heart is steady, he will not be afraid, until he sees his desire on his adversaries. He has distributed freely, he has

161

given to the poor; his righteousness endures for ever; his horn is exalted in honor.

Psalms 112:5–9 RSV

He that hath pity upon the poor lendeth unto the Lord; and that which he hath given will he pay him again.

Proverbs 19:17

32. The Corporate Grapevine

Where no wood is, there the fire goeth out: so where there is no talebearer, the strife ceaseth.

Proverbs 26:20

A wise man holds his tongue. Only a fool blurts out everything he knows; that only leads to sorrow and trouble.

Proverbs 10:14 TLB

Idle hands are the devil's workshop; idle lips are his mouthpiece. An evil man sows strife; gossip separates the best of friends.

Proverbs 16:27, 28 TLB

Have you heard of the new diet plan once hyped on ABC's "Good Morning, America"? David Hartman interviewed Joey Skaggs about this new diet regimen that essentially involves a team of strongmen who follow the dieter around and physically restrain him from eating.

Well, if you're interested and would like to give Joey Skaggs a call, don't. He'll laugh in your face, just like he did all the others who phoned him from all over the world. Skaggs, a Greenwich Village "media hoax artist," thinks it great fun to plant phony stories such as this new diet regimen and see how far the rumors spread. He is rarely disappointed, as the chagrined ABC officials learned when their interview story and subject were exposed.

The nuclear-plant disaster at Chernobyl serves as still another example, a much more serious one, of rumor run rampant. Although the Soviet Union didn't allow firsthand reporting on the incident, reporters, pressed by their bosses for a story—*any* story—came up with vastly inflated casualty figures of about two thousand. A sister rumor was that Soviet Union plants lacked the safety features found in all United States plants. Several weeks later, both rumors turned out to be false, but the corrections got very little media coverage.

Winston Churchill once claimed, "A lie gets halfway around the world before the truth puts on its boots." To bring it closer to the office, let's put it this way: Gossip gets to the employee lounge before the facts come through the computer cable.

Why is the business office such a fertile ground for gossip about other people's lives and the company's problems? For some, it's idleness; they have nothing more constructive to occupy their time. For others, sharing the latest about little-known situations makes them feel important. For still others, giving inside information wins friends. Those who gossip for such reasons lack self-esteem and need to find more appropriate ways to build their confidence.

Gossip has been well defined as the practice of putting two and two together and making five. Sometimes, even *listening* to others' gossip is what makes it five. Be careful about responding to gossip with comments such as the following:

"I can certainly see why you're upset" or "I don't blame you in the least" or "Well, I wondered why so-and-so didn't come into the meeting today. I guess that's why." Such responses are often assimilated into the gossiper's tale, and you are then cited during the next recitation.

Even if the gossiper and the listener don't suffer any personal consequences from getting involved in somebody else's conflict, other unanticipated harm may result.

In 1982, the Gulf Oil Chemical Company located in Baytown, Texas, was the victim of bomb threats and attempted extortion of $15 million. During the investigation by the company and FBI officials, rumors were rampant among workers about the contents of extortion letters mailed to Gulf:

- The money was to be parachuted from a company plane.
- The plant was selected because of its isolation.
- The extortionists warned that another plant—one closer to a residential area—would be a likely target for bombs if the demands were not met.
- The extortionists included three people or groups: someone who masterminded the plan, someone who built the devices, and someone who planted them. Corporate headquarters might also be a target.
- The extortionists told the Gulf officials that they would easily find the first five devices but would have difficulty with the last four (*Houston Chronicle*, October 3, 1982).

Can you imagine the unrest, the activity, and the cost involved in containing those various rumors—none of which was true—until the FBI finished its investigation and the matter came under closer examination in later court proceedings?

Even having the facts straight is no excuse for passing them on!

Almost every company has a similar story to tell. For years, a rumor has floated around that a portion of Procter & Gamble's profits is going to the church of satan. This story, often spread even in religious circles, has cost the company untold damage.

Even "harmless" gossip can produce sudden stress. After the first morning break in a seminar I was conducting for older employees at a client's site, attendees rumbled back into our meeting room quite alarmed. Rumor had just hit the twelfth floor that the company was about to be bought out. By the late afternoon break, the hostile-takeover rumors had four different companies supposedly moving to buy out the client organization. Needless to say, the older employees, worried about their retirement options, got little out of the seminar topic that day. All rumors later proved to be false.

The next time you're tempted to share a story, ask yourself: Has this story been verified? Will anybody or any situation be helped by my passing on this information? Will any person, project, or relationship be jeopardized by my passing on this information? What is my motive for talking or listening? When in doubt, leave it out.

Gossip is expensive; it costs character as well as hard dollars. The English author Francis Quarles concludes: "Where lies are easily admitted, the father of lies will not easily be kept out."

For Further Reflection:

Don't tell your secrets to a gossip unless you want them broadcast to the world.

Proverbs 20:19 TLB

A gossip goes around spreading rumors, while a trustworthy man tries to quiet them.

Proverbs 11:13 TLB

The words of a talebearer are as wounds, and they go down into the innermost parts of the belly.

Proverbs 26:22

33. Gratitude on This Gravy?

Give thanks in all circumstances; for this is the will of God in Christ Jesus for you.

1 Thessalonians 5:18 RSV

Keep your life free from love of money, and be content with what you have; for he has said, "I will never fail you nor forsake you."

Hebrews 13:5 RSV

They call it take-home pay because there's no other place you can afford to go with it.

Such quips are seemingly rather harmless, but some people become embittered by such sentiments. They use their paycheck as an excuse for lack of productivity on the job and even as an excuse for stealing from their employer.

Others, who would never think of actually stealing from an employer, nevertheless suffer from a "the grass is always greener on the other payroll" perspective. "And Joshua said,

Alas, O Lord God, wherefore hast thou at all brought this people over Jordan, to deliver us into the hand of the Amorites, to destroy us? would to God we had been content, and dwelt on the other side Jordan!'' (Joshua 7:7.)

Haven't we all known persons who left low-paying jobs for something else that they ultimately found inconvenient, stressful, and unfulfilling? Sometimes the new tasks, demands, and trade-offs aren't as easy to cope with as we first imagined. In other words, the green grass on the other side of the fence has to be mowed, too.

Aside from the grass-is-always-greener philosophy, another reason we tend to feel discontent with our wages involves our pride. The more prideful we are, the more we think we deserve. When asked how much they earn, employees often reply: "Twice what the boss thinks I'm worth and half what I deserve." It's very difficult for a proud individual to give an honest evaluation of what he or she contributes to the organization's efforts to reach its goals.

A focus on what we *lack*, rather than on what we *have*, is still another reason we feel discontent. There's an old story about the man who complained that he had no money to buy shoes until he met a man who had no feet.

We value such learning experiences about gratefulness for our children. A friend of mine recently was talking about his teenage daughter's reaction to a situation while on a youth mission trip. She had stayed with a poor family in the community where they were conducting Bible schools, and upon her return to her affluent home and parents, she tried hard to describe the depth of the poverty she had seen. "Did you know those poor people didn't even have light switches on the wall?" In all her eighteen years, she had never seen a naked light bulb hanging by its cord from the ceiling!

Perspective is everything. Don't you imagine God looks on our sheltered existence much the same way these parents looked on their daughter's experience?

We may not be the best-paid employee in the city, but we

are probably not the worst-paid, either. Perseverance and gratefulness may play as much a part in our lives as talent and reward.

At the age of thirty-eight, Johann Sebastian Bach had to compete with five others for the job of choirmaster at Saint Thomas Church, Leipzig. He got the job—not because of his already growing musical reputation, but because he alone agreed to teach Latin five days a week to elementary-age children in the church school!

Gratitude is not a matter of luck or talent or wealth. It's a mental attitude. Does your life seem to be one long, drawn-out sigh? If so, gratitude is the gravy that can make life's problems more palatable. Rather than a grumbling glare and a forward-looking prayer asking for more of God's blessings, perhaps we should glance backward and offer thanksgiving. Gratitude often becomes the root of many other virtues.

For Further Reflection:

Giving thanks always for all things unto God and the Father in the name of our Lord Jesus Christ.

Ephesians 5:20

. . . and what hast thou that thou didst not receive? . . .

1 Corinthians 4:7

Not that I complain of want; for I have learned, in whatever state I am, to be content. I know how to be abased, and I know how to abound; in any and all circumstances I have learned the secret of facing plenty and hunger, abundance and want. I can do all things in him who strengthens me.

Philippians 4:11–13 RSV

34. Greedy Piranhas

For the love of money is the root of all evil: which while some coveted after, they have erred from the faith, and pierced themselves through with many sorrows.

1 Timothy 6:10

Hell and destruction are never full; so the eyes of man are never satisfied.

Proverbs 27:20

And he said unto them, Take heed, and beware of covetousness: for a man's life consisteth not in the abundance of the things which he possesseth.

Luke 12:15

You've heard it said that one can never be too rich or too thin. I dare to differ—at least on the rich part. You can be too rich when your jewelry spends more time in the bank's safe than on your body. You can be too rich when everything you own needs to be dry-cleaned. You can be too rich when your parakeets have breeding papers. You can be too rich when your chauffeurs must hire assistants. You can be too rich when your distant relatives read the daily obituary columns in your city's newspapers.

Most of us have a difficult time seriously drawing the line between enough and not enough. Perhaps the line forms around our *attitude* about money rather than the green stuff itself: Poverty will make you long for better food and clothes. Money will whet your appetite for luxuries. Greed will lead you to put the other person out of business.

Such are the attitudes often found on Wall Street among the likes of Dennis Levine and Ivan Boesky, who left quite a trail of greed. In May 1986, Levine, of Drexel Burnham Lambert, was charged with raking in $12.6 million on insider-trading deals. When he agreed to cooperate, others got in the line of fire. Ivan Boesky agreed to pay a $100 million penalty for trading on inside information and also began to name others. The list goes on and on.

What is the general public's attitude about such shenanigans? Well, if my daily phone calls are any indication, most people don't blink an eye. I continue to get weekly calls from brokers asking for my trust, confiding that they "have done really well for some of their clients," and promising to do the same for me. In fact, one broker even laughed off the Boesky-Levine scandal, implying that, if anything, it was helping his business.

Our marketplace is full of such "get while the getting's good," "dog eat dog," and "get rich quick" attitudes and schemes. They aren't all coming out of Wall Street.

One of the newest greed-for-the-common-man schemes being played in hotel rooms around the country is a game called Airplane. The idea is to set up seats to resemble a passenger plane. The game participants talk colleagues into paying $1,000 for a seat to join the game. As each new passenger joins the airplane, the others move up toward the pilot's seat. The object of the scheme is to reach the pilot's quarters and bail out with the whole bundle of money. The risky part is keeping the game going long enough to reach the front of the plane and get your loot.

Not only does greed lead people into such illegal pastimes that show no regard for their fellowman, it even damages or destroys their own families. Children and spouses have been sacrificed to the philosophy of "just a little more." Enough would bring the working parent and spouse home at dinnertime; greed brings him or her home much later. Enough means a five-day workweek; greed demands the weekend. In corporate America, we have many families molded around the office, rather than the job molded around the family.

Greed leads us to betray friendships. Many people have sacrificed lifelong friendships over money disputes. Rather than give up their "right" to a few thousand dollars, people have ended relationships and sacrificed friends that would have provided great comfort and security through the years.

Others have betrayed friendships simply by neglect. When work competes for time with playing, eating, and talking together, friends often decide that making an extra dollar is of more lasting value than friendship. I hear people regretfully mourn the loss of time spent with friends they used to have, blaming it on the excessive demands of a job. Yet, who is holding the reigns of that runaway career?

Greed compromises morals. Paul warned about false teachers and preachers in his day, people who told others what they wanted to hear, so they would be popular and well supported financially. In our modern office, greed demands that we make our smaller competitors beg for a living, turn a deaf ear to employees asking for fair wages, spurn any requests from charities, cheat on our taxes, sell inferior and unsafe products, and accept kickbacks for bid approvals.

News stories of highly salaried corporate or political figures being indicted for accepting a kickback of only a few thousand dollars often puzzled me. I was amazed that someone of wealth and position would risk so much for so little.

But it finally dawned on me that logic is not at work in such matters; greed is. Only out-of-control greed (if there's any such thing as greed under control) could push logic, much less morality, out of the way.

But greed leaves its most serious marks on our relationship with God. The only record we have of Jesus' anger was His condemnation of the money changers in the temple. Profit on the street was not enough for them; their love of money brought them right into the temple with their wares. The love of money reared its face at least three times at Jesus' death. Judas took his thirty pieces of silver, the soldiers cast lots for His garments at the cross, and soldiers at the graveside took their bribe to lie about His resurrection.

Men today are still controlled and compromised by their greed. The Bible has more to say about money than it has to say about either heaven or hell. Shouldn't we give greed closer scrutiny, even if our business isn't located on Wall Street?

For Further Reflection:

Yea, they are greedy dogs which can never have enough, and they are shepherds that cannot understand: they all look to their own way, every one for his gain, from his quarter.

Isaiah 56:11

A faithful man shall abound with blessings: but he that maketh haste to be rich shall not be innocent. . . . He that hasteth to be rich hath an evil eye, and considereth not that poverty shall come upon him.

Proverbs 28:20, 22

One man gives freely, yet grows all the richer; another withholds what he should give, and only suffers want. A liberal man will be enriched, and one who waters will himself be watered. The people curse him who holds back grain, but a blessing is on the head of him who sells it.

Proverbs 11:24–26 RSV

35. Staying Flexible When You Stand on Absolutes

The good influence of godly citizens causes a city to prosper, but the moral decay of the wicked drives it downhill.

Proverbs 11:11 TLB

Ye are the light of the world. A city that is set on a hill cannot be hid. Neither do men light a candle, and put it under a bushel, but on a candlestick; and it giveth light unto all that are in the house. Let your light so shine before men, that they may see your good works, and glorify your Father which is in heaven.

Matthew 5:14–16

"Influence is the exhalation of character," observes Scottish clergyman W. M. Taylor. And Englishman George Bulwer notes, "A good man does good merely by living."

A restaurant owner in Irving, Texas, although he had been through difficult days, refused to recognize any need for God in his life. Because of his addiction to alcohol, he'd lost his home, family, and business. Finally, he was reduced to writing hot checks for his immediate physical needs, and as a result, was sentenced to several months in prison. When he returned to our community and was reunited with his family, the local pastor continued to send representatives to his door to share their faith. A converted drug addict, a converted alcoholic, and a converted exconvict all made their way to him, to try to say something that would influence him to accept God in his life and change his life-style. All to no avail.

Several years later, a young evangelist came to the church and shared his simple experience of growing up in a Christian home, being converted at an early age, and preaching the Gospel since the age of twenty. The restaurant owner responded and committed his life to God.

The church community was puzzled. Why had he not identified with and responded to the others, who had led an early life similar to his own? What had this young evangelist said that got through to him? The restaurant owner responded, "I always figured all these other guys, the addicts, had just turned over a new leaf. I figured it was only a matter of time until they were back in the gutter. But this guy told me about a God that had kept him away from all that garbage for his entire life. A God big enough to do that got my attention."

Most of us will never know how far the influence of a godly life reaches. The admirable character that philosophers have referred to can express itself many ways in the marketplace: by word, deed, or attitude.

I recently missed one of my chances. I was hurriedly scribbling on the flip chart in the conference room when a manager from the client organization stepped through the doorway behind me with this greeting: "Welcome back. We haven't seen you around in a while. How have you been this last year? What's the oil glut doing to your business?"

I proceeded to tell her in detail with, I'm afraid, a discouraged, defeated look and tone. When I finished my monologue through the doldrums, she responded, "Isn't that always the way it goes? When things really get going well, it's almost like there's a God up there who decides to zap you off your feet for a good laugh."

Her bitter retort and chuckle so startled me that I couldn't reply. Although she wasn't a Christian, to her way of thinking, my defeatist tale had just reinforced her erroneous view of God. How many times in the past had what I said or not said led people away from, not toward, God? The influence of idle words or unspoken words can't be underestimated.

But many people extend their realm of influence in the marketplace only to the negatives, the attitudes or activities of which they *don't* approve. That is, they're against office affairs, dishonesty in record keeping, wild partying, illegal wiretaps, Communism, lying, and profanity. That's all well and good.

But what are we Christians in the work force actually *for*? Are we initiating positive influences?

To paraphrase Galatians 5:14, are we showing love? Have we organized corporate tutoring programs for the disadvantaged? Are we writing company policies, devising campaigns, and soliciting donations for charity? Have we invited an unlovable colleague to lunch? Have we tried to restore a co-worker's destroyed reputation?

Are we influencing with joy? Do we have a congenial spirit? Do we add energy to the office? Do we inspire hope when our colleagues feel defeated?

Are we sowing peace? Do we listen to gossip or squelch it? Do we pass on good comments one colleague has said about another that might serve as a means of reconciliation? Do we actively try to resolve conflict, or simply choose to stay out of it?

Do we set an example of patience and gentleness? Are we the person others turn to if they have to ask for a repeat of instructions, or do others hide their mistakes from us, in fear of an angry, insulting outburst over the error? Do colleagues hate to be the ones to pass on bad news to us because of our harsh reactions? Do we encourage and provide for professional growth experiences for those we supervise?

Are we faithful? Can others count on us to keep our word when we make promises in meetings and on the telephone? Do we meet deadlines? Can others count on us to be the same to all people, showing no partiality? Can others count on our consistency in our moral choices?

Do we influence others by exemplifying self-control and moderation? Do we respect the body God has given us? Do we eat, rest, and exercise properly?

Even nature observes the effects of influence. As Pascal noted, "The least movement is of importance to all nature. The entire ocean is affected by a pebble." How much of your business environment do you affect for the better when you talk, act, and react within your company?

For Further Reflection:

Indeed all who desire to live a godly life in Christ Jesus will be persecuted, while evil men and impostors will go on from bad to worse, deceivers and deceived. But as for you, continue in what you have learned and have firmly believed, knowing from whom you learned it and how from childhood you have been acquainted with the sacred writings which are able to instruct you for salvation through faith in Christ Jesus.

2 Timothy 3:12–15 RSV

My son, if sinners entice thee, consent thou not.

Proverbs 1:10

36. Teaching an Old Employee New Tricks

What a shame—yes, how stupid!—to decide before knowing the facts! . . . The intelligent man is always open to new ideas. In fact, he looks for them.

Proverbs 18:13, 15 TLB

Through wisdom is an house builded; and by understanding it is established: And by knowledge shall the chambers be filled with all precious and pleasant riches. A wise man is strong; yea, a man of knowledge increaseth strength.

Proverbs 24:3–5

Available information now doubles every twenty months, according to John Naisbitt, author of the best-seller *Megatrends* and a periodic newsletter. Occasionally we hear those who extol ignorance and display false humility, as if they were virtues: "Now, jurors, I'm just an ignorant country lawyer, but I think. . . ." Some use ignorance as a common denominator: "I couldn't care less how this machine works, but. . . ."

Ignorance is never a virtue, and what you don't know can certainly hurt you.

In the last few years, we've heard the term *knowledge worker* bandied around a great deal. In fact, the knowledge worker—the employee who gathers, distributes, analyzes, and interprets information—is the fastest growing segment of the work population. But as you can see from the Scriptures cited above, the acquiring of knowledge has been important to individuals and society for a long time.

Only the emphasis has changed: The old philosopher advised, "Know thyself." The new philosopher advises, "Improve thyself."

According to a report by the American Society for Training and Development, employers spend an estimated $210 billion a year to train their workers. But even with the current trend to rush to night classes on subjects ranging from toe painting to physics, some businesspeople are still reluctant.

Because I'm in the corporate training and education business myself, I often hear two opposing viewpoints about on-the-job learning: Some perceive it as a perk, and some see it as a punishment. Not infrequently in supervisory-skills courses, time-management courses, or sales courses, participants saunter into the classroom with a bored scowl and comment: "My boss sent me. I don't know why he's got it in for me, or what I did wrong." Usually it doesn't take too long to figure out why the boss sent him! That attitude about learning usually explains a multitude of other problems on the job.

Learning is a lifelong effort for everyone. But to the wise businessperson, learning is a job perk. In fact, some companies recruit cream-of-the-crop employees by emphasizing their educational-development programs. IBM is one such company, devoting more dollars to training than any other

United States organization outside the federal government. According to Ray Abuzayyad, president of IBM's General Products Division, speaking at the American Society of Training and Development's national convention, on the average, each IBM employee receives ten days of education a year. And every manager is *required* to take five days of training each year.

It has been said that we are all ignorant—only on different subjects. There is no shame in ignorance on matters that we've not been exposed to. Disgrace follows only when we're made aware of our ignorance and refuse to snuff it out with knowledge.

When employees stop learning, they start a downward slide. When leaders quit learning about things around them and lose their sense of awareness about new trends, they become closed minded. To survive, they must hire consultants or new employees to come into their organizations and give them newer, broader perspectives on problems.

As 1 Corinthians 8:2 warns, most often when we think we have all the answers, we soon find that we don't even know all the right questions! The more knowledge we gain, the more aware we become of how much knowledge there is to master. If you've ever sat across the conference table from a know-it-all, that very attitude confirms your creeping uneasiness that you probably need to check further for more information. When someone becomes totally closed to new ideas, we begin to see the limit of his or her knowledge.

Most of us have quoted Alexander Pope on occasion: "A little learning is a dangerous thing." We don't have to be nearly so cautious of the deceptive employee as we do of the honest worker who simply doesn't know what he's doing—and goes about it with fervor!

Along with the Bible's admonition about the virtue of acquiring knowledge, we also need to keep in mind certain precautions.

First, be cautious about any pride over acquired knowledge. Treat knowledge like an automobile. When someone needs a ride, pull it out of the garage and take them where they need to go. But there's no need to drive down to the bus stop every twenty minutes and honk your horn at the pedestrians waiting in the rain. Learning and humility complement each other.

A second precaution: Don't be duped by the simplicity of knowledge and wisdom. Some of the greatest truths are so simple that we tend to downplay them or forget them until they slap us in the face again in the midst of difficulty. Consider: "Haste makes waste." "The love of money is the root of all evil." "A person is known by the company he keeps." "Pride goes before a fall." Don't let the simplicity of knowledge downplay its significance to you.

A final precaution about knowledge: Be careful to gain knowledge of the right things. Psalms 111:10 tells us the fear of the Lord is the beginning of wisdom. And as the Apostle Paul admonishes in 2 Timothy 2:15, we gain that fear and knowledge of the Lord through Bible study and contemplation of the truths exposed there.

It has been said that knowledge is power; knowledge of the ways of the Lord allows us access to both the world's knowledge and God's power.

For Further Reflection:

Buy truth, and do not sell it; buy wisdom, instruction, and understanding.

Proverbs 23:23 RSV

An intelligent mind acquires knowledge, and the ear of the wise seeks knowledge.

Proverbs 18:15 RSV

Take my instruction instead of silver, and knowledge rather than choice gold.

Proverbs 8:10 RSV

First Thing Monday Morning

Teach me good judgment and knowledge, for I believe in thy commandments.

Psalms 119:66 RSV

Study to shew thyself approved unto God, a workman that needeth not to be ashamed, rightly dividing the word of truth.

2 Timothy 2:15

37. Listening and Other Lowly Habits

Don't talk so much. You keep putting your foot in your mouth. Be sensible and turn off the flow! When a good man speaks, he is worth listening to, but the words of fools are a dime a dozen.

Proverbs 10:19, 20 TLB

An unreliable messenger can cause a lot of trouble. Reliable communication permits progress.

Proverbs 13:17 TLB

In early 1987, M. David Lowe Personnel Agency surveyed two hundred Houston workers, asking them to suggest New Year's resolutions for their bosses. The most frequently mentioned resolution was, "Communicate more with staff." The employees got even more specific on various aspects of communication when they gave other suggestions: Learn to listen, be more open to staff suggestions, give more praise, learn more about what your employees do, learn your employees' names. Most of their answers have to do with listening, not talking.

Although we often think of communication as a fifty-fifty proposition, we're usually splitting the percentage between people: 50 percent effort on one person's part and 50 percent effort on the other person's part. But consider that percentage solely in your own communication patterns: 50 percent talking and 50 percent listening. It takes skill in both areas to be adequate on the job.

Perhaps we don't hear God when He speaks to us because we don't get much practice in listening to other people. Jesus knew when to talk and when to listen. Coming into the district of Caesarea Philippi, He asked his disciples, "Whom do men say that I the Son of man am?" (Matthew 16:13). You'll notice that Jesus didn't begin by lecturing on His identity. Instead, He asked a question. What had they observed and absorbed by being with Him during His ministry? What opinion did the crowds have of Him? In other words, He was getting feedback, checking His perception of their understanding.

With the Samaritan woman at the well, He used a different technique. He communicated His identity to her by telling her that He was the Living Water and the possessor of eternal life (John 4).

The writer of Ecclesiastes tells us that there's a time for both sides of communication, a time to speak and a time to keep silent. But I have a hunch that most of us spend far too much time talking and not enough time listening. Do you recognize any of the following attitudes in your own listening habits?

- "I don't understand." (You don't pay attention because you think the subject is too complex. What's more, you're not interested enough to put forth the effort to learn.)
- "I know what you mean." (You assume you know what

the talker thinks or feels, and you don't bother to check to see if your perception is correct.)

- "I've got my mind made up." (You've already made up your mind about the issue, no matter what the other person says. During the talker's effort to express an opinion, you're concentrating on how you'll present your own views when he or she is finished. In fact, the few details you do catch, you plan to use as ammunition in your rebuttal.)
- "That's off the wall." (You make a snap judgment, refusing to consider unusual ideas, plans, opinions, or feelings.)
- "I don't want to get involved." (You mean, "Don't tell me your problems. I've got my own." We often divert the talker with, "Speaking of reports due, that reminds me, I need. . . .")
- "I don't like you." (You don't like the way someone dresses, walks, or sells shoes, so you're closed to anything the person has to say on any subject.)

Listening is not only beneficial to the person doing the talking; good listening habits are to our own advantage. The English dramatist and novelist Oliver Goldsmith observed: "Every absurdity has a champion to defend it, for error is always talkative." Perhaps an easy way to reduce our own error factor on the job is to talk less and listen more.

In the next business meeting that you conduct or attend, observe those around you, and see if you don't agree with the following observations:

Be always less willing to speak than to hear; what thou hearest, thou receivest; what thou speakest thou givest.— It is more glorious to give, but more profitable to receive.

Francis Quarles
English author

It is the characteristic of great wits to say much in few
words, so it is of small wits to talk much and say nothing.

La Rochefoucauld
French courtier

People who consider themselves great communicators often talk just because they can express themselves well, rather than because their ideas are sound and profitable.

If Jesus felt the need to ask questions and listen to His friends for feedback, how much more should we check our perceptions and improve ourselves by listening?

Here's how:

- Be aware of your own bad listening habits and attitudes.
- Be silent occasionally, to give others a chance to speak.
- Open the door for others with phrases like, "What do you think about . . . ?"
- Focus your whole body on listening; "be there," without shuffling papers or jiggling your keys while others speak.
- Ask questions when you don't understand.
- Ask questions to check that you really understood.
- Listen between the lines, to the feelings as well as the words.
- Express understanding.
- Summarize to yourself what the other person said and decide if you need to do something, change something, or improve something about yourself and the way you do business.

For Further Reflection:

Listen, son of mine, to what I say. Listen carefully.

Proverbs 4:20 TLB

My son, attend unto my wisdom, and bow thine ear to my understanding: That thou mayest regard discretion, and that thy lips may keep knowledge.

Proverbs 5:1, 2

Listening and Other Lowly Habits

I will hear what God the Lord will speak: for he will speak peace unto his people, and to his saints: but let them not turn again to folly.

Psalms 85:8

38. Just Sign on the Dotted Line . . . .

Son, if you endorse a note for someone you hardly know, guaranteeing his debt, you are in serious trouble. You may have trapped yourself by your agreement. Quick! Get out of it if you possibly can! Swallow your pride; don't let embarrassment stand in the way. Go and beg to have your name erased. Don't put it off. Do it now. Don't rest until you do. If you can get out of this trap you have saved yourself like a deer that escapes from a hunter, or a bird from the net.

Proverbs 6:1–5 TLB

Be sure you know a person well before you vouch for his credit! Better refuse than suffer later.

Proverbs 11:15 TLB

It is poor judgment to countersign another's note, to become responsible for his debts.

Proverbs 17:18 TLB

"Creditors have better memories than debtors; they are a superstitious sect, great observers of set days and times," Ben Franklin wryly noted. If you've ever lent money to an acquaintance, you'll note how lenders not only become clock-watchers and calendar watchers, but also behavior and attitude observers.

We see one of our debtors out eating pizza with his family on Tuesday night and wonder how he can afford it, owing us what he does. We phone his house, finding him still in bed in the morning, and pointedly remind him that we've been at work for hours.

Soon the borrower's attitude also begins to change with regard to his benefactor's generosity. English essayist Joseph Addison defines a moneylender with that guarded perspective: "He serves you in the present tense; he lends you in the conditional mood; keeps you in the subjunctive; and ruins you in the future!" Consider the movie version of the stereotypical Mr. Moneybags, who preys on the innocent by charging outrageous interest and calling in loans at the most inopportune times.

Whether you're the borrower or the lender, the loan changes the way both parties see each other forever. If you try to force the other person to pay, he or she becomes a sure enemy. If you don't ask for repayment, you may lose money you can't afford to squander, and become bitter.

Friendship most often falls by the wayside.

Another reason to pause before lending money to an acquaintance is the consideration that you may not really be helping the other person when you help him go into debt. That individual may continue to do business or live beyond his or her means. When the person falls into debt up to the eyeballs and begins to feel the pressure of the waves around him, he may not think of you as a lifeguard with a raft but rather as a big gust of wind, blowing him farther from shore.

And while endorsing someone's character can be embarrassing and unfruitful, endorsing another's credit can be downright expensive. In his younger days, my father agreed to a business partnership with a man who had always been good doing electrical repairs. My father signed a note and agreed to put up the first $500 to open the shop where the man would ply his part-time trade repairing TVs and radios. A few weeks later, the man left town with the money—before the store opened its doors.

Nothing tests character—the borrower's or the lender's—like one's handling of credit.

So what should you do when asked to lend money? If you can afford to do so, give it. Generosity is Godlike.

For Further Reflection:

Unless you have the extra cash on hand, don't countersign a note. Why risk everything you own? They'll even take your bed!

Proverbs 22:26, 27 TLB

The world's poorest credit risk is the man who agrees to pay a stranger's debts.

Proverbs 27:13 TLB

39. Participative Management and Micaiah

Without counsel plans go wrong, but with many advisers they succeed.

Proverbs 15:22 RSV

Pride leads to arguments; be humble, take advice and become wise.

Proverbs 13:10 TLB

We hear a lot today about Theory X and Theory Y managers. Theory X managers believe that employees are basically lazy and unmotivated, that they work solely for a paycheck as a reward, and that they have few creative ideas to contribute to the workplace. These managers conclude that such employees need authoritarian control and discipline.

Theory Y managers, on the other hand, believe that most workers are self-motivated, enjoy being productive, work for rewards other than a paycheck, and can contribute ideas on how to do their jobs better. They control themselves fairly well and work responsibly when given appropriate guidelines. These employees, Theory Y managers believe, need opportunities to grow and to participate in their own growth and that of their company.

Neither Theory X managers nor Theory Y managers are immune to mistakes. Authoritarian managers who listen to no one obviously ignore the Bible's admonition about the safety and assurance found by seeking many opinions before making decisions.

But Theory Y managers can make the equally egregious mistake of listening to the wrong people at the wrong times. In effect, they clue others to what they want them to say, and they don't even bother to ask those employees who might give contradictory opinions. In staff meetings, they're the kind who ask with a scowl, "Does anybody have any *serious* objections to proceeding as I've outlined?"

Such was the case with King Ahab and the prophet Micaiah (*see* 2 Chronicles 18). For three years, Syria and Israel had not gone to war. But during Judean King Jehoshaphat's visit to King Ahab of Israel, King Ahab began to grumble to his court officials about something not being right in the kingdom. Syria still occupied Ramoth-gilead, one of their cities. He asked his ally King Jehoshaphat if he were willing to join him in the effort to reclaim the city. King Jehoshaphat agreed, with the caution that they'd better ask the Lord about the outcome first.

When King Ahab asked his four hundred false prophets about the decision, they said, in effect, "Go for it. God'll give you a sure victory."

But King Jehoshaphat wasn't satisfied. "Aren't we leaving out somebody? Isn't there somebody else we should ask?"

Reluctantly, King Ahab called in Micaiah. When he was first asked, Micaiah agreed with the other prophets that King

Ahab would be successful in battle, just as the messenger sent to get him had advised him.

But we'll at least have to give the king credit for realizing when his man was giving advice under pressure. He gave him "permission" to really speak what he was thinking and got the opposite advice: The word from the Lord was *not* to go to battle.

Do you think King Ahab was glad to be warned of his impending death? No. He had Micaiah thrown in prison to survive on bread and water until he returned victorious. Wishful thinking. Despite all his precautions to thwart the prophet's warning, King Ahab died in battle.

Several business truths shout from this story: First, as the proverb says, seek advisers.

And where are those advisers who can give insight into our decisions? Often right under our noses.

According to 7,800 responses to a national survey sponsored by *Working Woman* magazine (October 1986), top managers are making a big mistake in the 1980s. To keep good employees, they have focused on the growth industries' allure of glittering compensation packages.

The ironic, surprising finding of that study was that instead of big salaries and stock options, employees are more concerned about how management treats them. These 7,800 career women responding to the survey insisted that the work climate, standards for performance, and the work itself are what really make them feel good about their jobs. In other words, they like being allowed to participate in management decisions and challenging work.

But besides the value of allowing employees to be advisers on the job, bosses have to be careful about surrounding themselves with yes-men and -women and suffering from "group think." That is, they need to be careful not to foster an atmosphere where everybody feels pressure to fit into the mold and where the least risky common denominator among a group dictates the course of action.

The overwhelming evidence is that businesspeople do care about the climate of their workplace, do want to be seen as individuals and challenged to take part in decision making, and do care about the results. The job of all of us, whether we are bosses or subordinates, is to ask for ideas from our co-workers and then evaluate those ideas fairly.

"Good intelligence is nine-tenths of any battle," Napoleon said. Businesspeople who don't recognize the contribution of their co-workers to their own success and the organization's goals are dangerous people to have on the job.

For Further Reflection:

Don't go ahead with your plans without the advice of others; don't go to war until they agree.
Proverbs 20:18 TLB

40. Sure Job Had Patience, But He Never Worked *Here*

But they that wait upon the Lord shall renew their strength; they shall mount up with wings as eagles; they shall run, and not be weary; and they shall walk, and not faint.

Isaiah 40:31

Dear brothers, is your life full of difficulties and temptations? Then be happy, for when the way is rough, your patience has a chance to grow. So let it grow, and don't try to squirm out of your problems. For when your patience is finally in full bloom, then you will be ready for anything, strong in character, full and complete.

James 1:2–4 TLB

With patience a ruler may be persuaded, and a soft tongue will break a bone.

Proverbs 25:15 RSV

195

"There is as much difference between genuine patience and sullen endurance, as between the smile of love and the malicious gnashing of the teeth," insisted W. S. Plumer, nineteenth-century clergyman. While we wait and work, patience does not mean that we have to feel careless, cold-hearted, and condemned to nonproductivity or failure.

Neither is patience a state of indifference, when we don't care about an outcome and consequently feel no urgency for change or action.

Actually, patience is a positive state, an action rather than a reaction. "The two powers which in my opinion constitute a wise man are those of bearing and forbearing," claimed Epictetus, the Roman philosopher. Bearing is choosing to work under pressure, and forbearing is a conscious decision to extend patience to others, to accomplish objectives with whatever they offer or fail to offer.

Patience can often be power. With patience and power, the caterpillar becomes a moth. The patience of the negotiator in making his proposal builds a winning strategy. In fact, nothing marks an amateur so much as impatience in any kind of business effort—negotiations in particular. The Bible warns us not to rush into different business endeavors without preparing and counting the costs: "A wise man is cautious and avoids danger; a fool plunges ahead with great confidence" (Proverbs 14:16 TLB).

Patience provides us with choices. After taking the dive, it's difficult to switch directions in midair.

Patience also improves our logic. We hear people in pressure situations say, "I can't think on my feet," or, more aptly said, "I can't think under heat." In a rush situation, we often make strategic business errors, failing to see pitfalls along the path and even hurting people and relationships along the way to disaster. Patience allows time, circumstances, and other advisers to take off our blinders.

Patience improves our health. It promotes control of our own lives and attitudes, thereby our blood pressure and energy level. We have all heard about Type A personalities and the kinds of stress these people create for themselves and others. Signs of impatience are all around us. Impatient people:

- Walk up escalators
- Jab at close-door buttons on elevators
- Hurump and curse in the supermarket line
- Ask questions without waiting for answers
- Glare at their watches without noting the time

Stress-management experts have devised several exercises to improve our patience level as well as our physical health. When you go into a restaurant with friends, force yourself to be the last person to finish eating. Or in freeway traffic, force yourself to drive at the speed limit in the right-hand lane. Again, remember that patience is an action and a reaction.

Patience increases awareness. We begin to notice people around us, rather than being totally involved in getting on with our own lives. We think of things to say to them and become aware of the time and attention we could lavish on them. In so doing, we make their lives different and enrich ourselves in the process.

Patience makes us more tolerant of ourselves. We can't become more patient of other people without some of that patience lapping back onto us. We permit ourselves not to always be the first one through with a project, not to always arrive first at staff meetings. We forgive ourselves when we make "stupid" mistakes.

Finally, patience deepens our trust in God. According to the world, seeing is believing. According to God, believing is seeing. We learn that God's delays are not necessarily denials; we learn to give Him time to act on our behalf.

Many times God must see us the way we see TV sitcoms. We see the hero and the heroine, longing for each other's phone call, continue to miss each other. The heroine calls, and the hero is in the shower; by the time he gets to the phone, the ringing has stopped. We viewers feel that misconnection. Often because of our impatience in waiting for God's properly timed answers, we give up on Him and take the wrong action ourselves.

Although patience may be hard to define, we know the attitude or action when we see it:

- Patience indulges the meeting clown.
- Patience courteously asks for corrections.
- Patience avoids sulking while waiting for a return call.
- Patience investigates before investing.
- Patience permits others to smile when you yourself cry.
- Patience prays rather than pouts.

As Swiss theologian Johann Lavater reminds us: "He surely is most in need of another's patience, who has none of his own."

For Further Reflection:

For ye have need of patience, that, after ye have done the will of God, ye might receive the promise.

Hebrews 10:36

But thou, O man of God, flee these things; and follow after righteousness, godliness, faith, love, patience, meekness.

1 Timothy 6:11

For examples of patience in suffering, look at the Lord's prophets. We know how happy they are now because they stayed true to him then, even though they suffered greatly for it. Job is an example of a man who continued to trust the Lord in sorrow; from his experiences we can see how the Lord's plan finally ended in good, for he is full of tenderness and mercy.

James 5:10 TLB

41. Building Bigger Barns

We should make plans—counting on God to direct us.

Proverbs 16:9 TLB

A prudent man foresees the difficulties ahead and prepares for them; the simpleton goes blindly on and suffers the consequences.

Proverbs 22:3 TLB

Any enterprise is built by wise planning, becomes strong through common sense, and profits wonderfully by keeping abreast of the facts.

Proverbs 24:3, 4 TLB

We can make our plans, but the final outcome is in God's hands.

Proverbs 16:1 TLB

Look here, you people who say, "Today or tomorrow we are going to such and such a town, stay there a

year, and open up a profitable business." How do
you know what is going to happen tomorrow? For
the length of your lives is as uncertain as the morn-
ing fog—now you see it; soon it is gone. What you
ought to say is, "If the Lord wants us to, we shall
live and do this or that." Otherwise you will be
bragging about your own plans, and such self-con-
fidence never pleases God.

James 4:13–16 TLB

Who could have known that the oil crisis of the 1970s
would turn into an oil glut a mere ten years later? Who could
have predicted the breakup of AT&T and the influx of multitudes of long-distance services? Who among us sensed that
Ronald Reagan's landslide victory would turn into one of the
biggest foreign-policy fiascoes of the presidency? Before they
heard the rumblings in the ground, who could have forecast
the date of the earthquakes in Mexico City and Ecuador that
killed thousands?

Few would argue that we will always have unexpected
political, financial, and natural upheavals in the world. But
does that mean we as businesspeople should not plan for our
future? That we should not make plans to open a branch
office tomorrow? That we should not fund research on a cure
for cancer? That we should not further our personal education or expand our experience to acquire a better future?

Just what is the relationship between the Scriptures that
tell us to plan for the future and those that caution against
spending our money before we make it and presuming upon
the length of our days?

According to the Small Business Administration, the majority of all new businesses fail within the first five years.
That is not to say that a particular business idea was weak,
but simply that people who immediately grab an idea and
run with it often fail to match their product or service to the

right market, or even to their own personal goals and qualifications for the job. Additionally, they find they're without adequate staff or financing. Planning is no small matter.

Likewise with the large corporation. We have back-orders on Christmas toys. We build factories for manufacturing a new hoola-hoop, and then see them sit idle when the trend passes as quickly as it descended. We see advertising for products that are never produced. We must return recalled autos to the dealer because someone didn't take the time to make all the proper safety tests. Signs of poor planning sit everywhere.

Yet few would disagree that planning is a must; it forces us to devote regular, directed time to the future. We must ask ourselves what valuable information or experience we should glean from any situation for application in the future. How should the current events change the way we think about our product or service? What opportunities do these events or circumstances offer for the way we do business? Planning makes tasks easier, reduces confusion, saves time, and gives everyone direction.

Yes, planning makes good business sense. And often the best planning is simply doing the present tasks well, with an eye toward duty and detail.

But to posture ourselves between planning and presumption, we should consider the proper attitude about both. Augustine said it best: "God will not suffer man to have a knowledge of things to come; for if he had prescience of his prosperity, he would be careless; and if understanding of his adversity, he would be despairing and senseless."

Too much focus on a dark future creates worry. We fail to live today to its advantage and find little satisfaction in the small victories if we have a sense of impending doom. In the face of prosperity and success, we stand with stooped shoulders, as if braced for a timber falling across our backs.

On the other hand, presuming on a promising and prosperous future makes us self-reliant rather than God-reliant. We act carelessly toward our fellowman and disregard our duty to make the world a better place. What was once faith in God's providence becomes confidence in our own reasoning and expertise. And with that confidence comes pride and selfishness—the very opposites of Christlikeness in our lives.

Ben Franklin offered these observations about the part God's will plays in our planning: "The longer I live, the more convincing proofs I see of this truth, that God governs in the affairs of man; and if a sparrow cannot fall to the ground without His notice, is it probable that an empire can rise without His aid?"

Trust, yes. Be anxious, no. Plan, yes. Presume, no.

For Further Reflection:

A wise man thinks ahead; a fool doesn't, and even brags about it!

Proverbs 13:16 TLB

For which of you, intending to build a tower, sitteth not down first, and counteth the cost, whether he have sufficient to finish it? Lest haply, after he hath laid the foundation, and is not able to finish it, all that behold it begin to mock him, Saying, This man began to build, and was not able to finish.

Luke 14:28–30

The plans of the diligent lead surely to abundance, but every one who is hasty comes only to want.

Proverbs 21:5 RSV

Riches can disappear fast. And the king's crown doesn't stay in his family forever—so watch your business interests closely. Know the state of your flocks and your herds; then there will be lamb's wool enough for clothing, and goat's milk enough for food for all your household after the hay is harvested, and the new crop appears, and the mountain grasses are gathered in.

Proverbs 27:23–27 TLB

42. James, John, and Power Politics

For promotion and power come from nowhere on earth, but only from God. He promotes one and deposes another.

Psalms 75:6, 7 TLB

Did your parents ever leave the house for an evening or for a few days and put an older brother or sister in charge of you during their absence? Were you angry or pleased at the new authority?

Have you ever thought about why the Apostles James and John's quest for authority and power made the other disciples angry (Mark 10:35–45)? Whether James and John got to be hotshots really had little to do with the other ten. Or did it?

What is it about another's power that disturbs us on the job?

Power magnifies one's true character. Authority often brings out the littleness in people. Plutarch observed: "There is no stronger test of a man's real character than power and authority, exciting as they do every passion, and discovering every latent vice."

Many of us have made such an observation around the office. We know of bosses who, at the beginning of each year, whip out their calendars to record their vacations first and announce to everybody else that they should work around those times, regardless: regardless of another's child's graduation, an ill mother's planned birthday visit, or a long-planned trip with a spouse. We see managers whose greed leads them to make short-term profits at the expense of long-term benefits for the stockholders. We hear bosses pull rank to settle conflicts, rather than get to the bottom of an issue.

But just as power brings out the pettiness or vice in some, it brings out the best in others. Abraham could have chosen the most fertile fields for his stock and set Lot packing; however, he allowed his nephew first choice and took the leftover land for himself. Few in the business world follow his example when given the power to do otherwise.

The disciples may have become angry over James and John's request out of fear of the character traits that would rise to the surface with those two in charge.

Or, perhaps the other ten's attitude turned on simple jealousy.

You'll notice that when Jesus asked the two disciples if they were able to handle the responsibility that went with the power they sought, they answered with great confidence, "We are able." Many times we look with envy at those in positions of power and feel equally capable. But perhaps we'd do well to take a closer look at what power entails.

Power can be pain. Power can mean having to choose between two bad alternatives. A friend of mine recently had some difficult years, financially, resulting in his family having to sell their house and move into a less-expensive one. With tears in his eyes, he told me of a bigger regret: He had just had to terminate the employment of a dear friend who had worked for him for seventeen years.

Those in a place of power do not always face decisions with such grave consequences; nevertheless, few are easy.

A friend of mine who manages an office of eighteen people lamented to me that she hadn't been able to get to the dentist with her painful tooth. When I asked her why she hadn't taken off work early on Friday afternoon, she explained her choices. Two other employees had already scheduled the day for vacation. Another had to go to school to meet with a child's teacher. Another felt as though she were coming down with the flu. Another got a call from the school, asking her to pick up a sick child. Another had asked to leave early to catch a flight out of town to join a spouse at a business conference. With company policy saying that no more than three could be away at once, she had a hard choice about whose claim was more urgent or fair. And, of course, she canceled her own dentist appointment.

Power derived from a position of authority is not without its problems. Yet, some still strive for that magic wand of authority. James and John hoped to gain such power by their position as Jesus' "right-hand men." Power still comes to many people through their position in the corporate hierarchy, and that power is theirs to use for the benefit of all concerned, or to use to demean others and magnify their own pettiness.

But don't confuse such positional power with personal power. Although we don't all have our chance at the positional power bestowed by a corporate title, we all can have personal power.

Business management consultants and career experts often admonish fast trackers who want to get things done to forget the published chain of command and learn who has the real power. That real power has usually surfaced because of a person's moral character, ability to achieve results, and attachment to a good or great purpose.

Although authority possessed by virtue of one's paycheck,

title, or influential parents or friends can't be pushed aside, the most powerfully effective people possess personal power; that is, they have energy, insight, and ideas. With their confidence and zeal, they inspire others to see visions, to pursue excellence, and to sacrifice for the common good and a greater purpose. Having inspired, they communicate clear directives through personal example.

Always seek to develop personal power rather than positional power. Strive to be a leader that people would follow, if given a choice.

For Further Reflection:

And James and John, the sons of Zebedee, came forward to him, and said to him, "Teacher, we want you to do for us whatever we ask of you." And he said to them, "What do you want me to do for you?" And they said to him, "Grant us to sit, one at your right hand and one at your left, in your glory." But Jesus said to them, "You do not know what you are asking. Are you able to drink the cup that I drink, or to be baptized with the baptism with which I am baptized?" And they said to him, "We are able." And Jesus said to them, "The cup that I drink you will drink; and with the baptism with which I am baptized, you will be baptized; but to sit at my right hand or at my left is not mine to grant, but it is for those for whom it has been prepared." And when the ten heard it, they began to be indignant at James and John. And Jesus called them to him and said to them, "You know that those who are supposed to rule over the Gentiles lord it over them, and their great men exercise authority over them. But it shall not be so among you; but whoever would be great among you must be your servant, and whoever would be first among you must be slave of all. For the Son of man also came not to be served but to serve, and to give his life as a ransom for many."

Mark 10:35–45 RSV

43. Pride: Did I Ever Tell You About the Time . . . ?

What are you so puffed up about? What do you have that God hasn't given you? And if all you have is from God, why act as though you are so great, and as though you have accomplished something on your own?

1 Corinthians 4:7 TLB

And I will break the pride of your power; and I will make your heaven as iron, and your earth as brass.

Leviticus 26:19

A man's pride shall bring him low: but honour shall uphold the humble in spirit.

Proverbs 29:23

For I say, through the grace given unto me, to every man that is among you, not to think of himself more highly than he ought to think; but to think soberly,

*according as God hath dealt to every man the mea-
sure of faith.*

Romans 12:3

*There is one thing worse than a fool, and that is a
man who is conceited.*

Proverbs 26:12 TLB

*By humility and the fear of the Lord are riches, and
honour, and life.*

Proverbs 22:4

Take your pulse on pride:

- Do you enjoy controlling access to people or information?
- Do you take pride in being able to give orders to others?
- Do you enjoy approving or rejecting others' plans?
- Do you keep a mental checklist of how your job skills rate in comparison to others?
- At performance appraisal time, do you wish you knew how everyone else was rated in comparison to you?
- Do you consider your bank account to be a good measure of your success as a person?
- Do you ever have the urge to tell someone else how much you earn or how much your business is worth?
- Do you enjoy throwing your weight around as a buyer because you are a large account?
- Do you spend more than you can really afford on transportation, clothes, jewelry, hair, and personal-care items?
- Have you ever gotten a job because of your looks? Are you aware that physically attractive people are often considered to be brighter, more personable, and more capable than their less-attractive colleagues? Does this fact make you feel pride?

The causes of pride flourish in the workplace due to the very nature of the role our jobs play in defining our lives and success, as measured by man. Pride comes from control, power, skill, accomplishments, men's praise, wealth, and appearance—all matters often noted on the job. In fact, twice a year in formal appraisals, employees are asked to account for many of these things in their past performance and are rated on how they measure up.

If the previous questions lead you to discover that you do have seeds (or great big vines) of pride in your life, what can you expect in your job?

According to the Scriptures, pride leads to conflict. Someone's rights will always be in danger of violation: parking rights, telephone rights, space rights, schedule rights, confidentiality rights, cafeteria rights, meeting-invitation rights. There will be much pettiness, argument, and sullenness.

Pride causes confidence in ourselves rather than in God and presumption of the future. We begin to feel that we can make it with or without God. We assume that our security is in our accomplishments and job and, therefore, under our control.

Pride causes mutterings and complaints against God. We begin to ask questions such as: "How come I didn't get the same promotion as Joe?" "How dare God do this to me?" "What did I ever do to deserve this?" "Why am I working harder than anybody around here? Look where it gets me!" In other words, we decide that God isn't fair.

Pride causes us to look down on other people, par-ticularly those who are more spiritual than we are and those who are poorer. We feel superior to the person at the next desk and come to such conclusions as, "He's a real fanatic about religion, isn't he?" "He takes the interpretation of the Bible a little too far to be practical, doesn't he?" "Her hard luck is really her own fault. She should have known better." "These employees don't really expect more money; after all, they've always lived hand-to-mouth." "I got a good job and edu-cated myself. Why can't she?"

Pride leads to self-deceit and blindness about our own shortcomings: "The company should really be grateful that they have me. Not many people work as hard and know the job as well as I do." We gloss over the seriousness of weaknesses pointed out in our performance appraisals. We tend to blame others—the secretary, the marketing department, the "corporate culture"—for the projects that don't turn out as well as we had planned. We tend to turn positive-thinking tenets into self-justification for stagnation: "I focus on what I do well; the rest doesn't matter."

Finally, unhalted pride eventually brings us down. The payoff is humiliation. Awards begin to go to someone else. Senior management passes us by for bonuses and promotions. Profits turn to losses. Looks and good health fail. The truth of our own shortcomings and failures come to the light of day. Others look to us as an example of what *not* to do.

Those who shun God's humility must soon learn to live with their own humiliation. If you doubt the results of pride on the basis of what you see in your office today, tune in to the careers of the proud twenty years down the road.

For Further Reflection:

Every one that is proud in heart is an abomination to the Lord: though hand join in hand, he shall not be unpunished.

Proverbs 16:5

The fear of the Lord is to hate evil: pride, and arrogancy, and the evil way, and the froward mouth, do I hate.

Proverbs 8:13

Humility and reverence for the Lord will make you both wise and honored.

Proverbs 15:33 TLB

Better it is to be of an humble spirit with the lowly, than to divide the spoil with the proud.

Proverbs 16:19

Toward the scorners he is scornful, but to the humble he shows favor. The wise will inherit honor, but fools get disgrace.

Proverbs 3:34, 35 RSV

44. Priorities: Seeking the Kingdom Second

But seek ye first the kingdom of God, and his righteousness; and all these things shall be added unto you.

Matthew 6:33

No man can serve two masters: for either he will hate the one, and love the other; or else he will hold to the one, and despise the other. Ye cannot serve God and mammon.

Matthew 6:24

A double minded man is unstable in all his ways.

James 1:8

Two vice-presidents were recently discussing solutions to their difficulties in getting project funding. During the era of merger mania, their company had been bought out three times during a two-year period. As a result, the rank and file manager never knew who would have final approval of his or her budget requests.

In the past, one VP explained, their managers wrote up a simple purpose-and-necessity statement that basically said, "we need money to do repairs," and they got what they wanted. But with the latest buyout, things had changed. Past priorities had been repair and maintenance; the new management's priorities were expansion and government compliance. Needless to say, the managers were having a difficult time getting their budgets approved.

You've possibly experienced your own difficulties with changing priorities and the confusion such scenarios create on the job. Employees feel their efforts have been wasted, they taste defeat before they've even begun a project, and their enthusiasm for the next new idea slides several notches down the scale.

If confusion results from double mindedness on the job, there's little wonder at the upheavals we feel when our whole being—our relationships, our energy, our time—constantly seesaws on changing priorities.

One month, we decide to devote more time to our family, so we arrive home by 6:00 each evening and stay there until bedtime. The next month, we find ourselves attending this or that professional meeting or bowling with the league almost every evening.

The following month, we feel that God is asking us to devote more time to Him, so we volunteer to teach a Bible study class. Three months later, we give it up because our "business is too demanding."

The next month, we hear a missionary's plea for food for a ravaged country, and we pledge fifty dollars a month toward that goal. The following month, our kids need an extra jacket, and we wonder how we ever thought we could spare the fifty dollars in the first place.

Double-mindedness unravels relationships, wrecks budgets, wastes time and effort, and douses us with guilt and defeat.

So how do we become single-minded?

Not all children, of course, grow up in a household like Joshua's, where the father made the declaration, "But as for me and my house, we will serve the Lord." Some of us did grow up where that principle was taught—even in the small matters. My brother and I didn't study for exams or play with our teams if those events conflicted with worship times. We didn't hold back the tenth of our allowance just because we lacked a quarter to buy a favorite toy. Although we as kids didn't always have our druthers about the situation, our priorities were set for us by godly parents.

Adulthood and business, however, have brought us more choices, as well as chances for misjudgment and shuffled priorities. Sometimes I think it's unfortunate that we adults don't always have a Moses to make a circle, an Elijah to build an altar, or a Joshua to draw a line. Stepping inside the circle, up to the altar, or across the line would force us into clear-cut action or into inaction.

Most of the time, it's the absence of that clear-cut line that creates our difficulty and our stress.

"Conquering Stress," a KJ software package, leads users to take stock of the stress factors in their lives. The program begins with a personal-inventory quiz asking users to rank the importance of various relationships, events, times, and possessions in their lives. After that open-ended self-assessment quiz, users respond to another quiz about how they *actually* spend their time, how they work, and how they relate to people. Many users are quite surprised to see a comparison of their answers from the two quizzes.

Simply put, users learn that what they *say* is important to them is *not* shown by where they actually spend their time and money. That discrepancy is what causes stress.

One way to make our lives stable, and therefore less stressful, is to make them one-directional, to hammer out our priorities once and for all. As Disraeli put it: "The secret of success is constancy to purpose." That is, our purpose, or our priorities, must be determined long before we have to face any everyday decisions about actions, time, or money. When those tough decisions come, then it's simply a matter of seeing how they match up to the priorities we've already outlined for our lives and business.

Are God's priorities and our personal priorities in making money always contradictory? Certainly not. The Bible, however, does outline the appropriate whys behind our drive to make money. One proper motive is to give to God and others. A second proper motive is to provide for our family's needs. A third is to provide for our future needs.

Most of us, if we're honest, are all too well acquainted with the wrong motives: greed, pride, and envy. We have moved from need to greed in the acquiring of things. We are proud of the wealth we've earned by our own hard work or expertise. We envy the Joneses and feel the ego need to wear, eat, maintain, drive, mow, or sit in just what they do.

Such inappropriate motives for working put us in a continually stressful situation. We're not doing what we know, believe, and insist is our first priority. But if we seek God's priorities—fellowship with Him, time and money invested in His work, and attention to our families—the leftovers we toss toward financing our life-styles will always be adequate. God promised it; we can count on it. Bringing our priorities into line with God's proves to be the only sensible, stressless, satisfying step toward true success.

For Further Reflection:

Love not the world, neither the things that are in the world. If any man love the world, the love of the Father is not in him. For all that is in the world, the lust of the flesh, and the lust of the eyes, and the pride of life, is not of the Father, but is of the world. And the world passeth away, and the lust thereof: but he that doeth the will of God abideth for ever.

1 John 2:15–17

I know thy works, that thou art neither cold nor hot: I would thou wert cold or hot. So then because thou art lukewarm, and neither cold nor hot, I will spue thee out of my mouth.

Revelation 3:15, 16

45. Productivity: Ask Not What Your Organization Can Do for You; Ask What You Can Do for Your Organization

Whatsoever thy hand findeth to do, do it with thy might. . . .

Ecclesiastes 9:10

A lazy fellow is a pain to his employers—like smoke in their eyes or vinegar that sets the teeth on edge.

Proverbs 10:26 TLB

Hard work means prosperity; only a fool idles away his time.

Proverbs 12:11 TLB

He that is faithful in that which is least is faithful also in much: and he that is unjust in the least is unjust also in much. If therefore ye have not been faithful in the unrighteous mammon, who will commit to your trust the true riches? And if ye have not been faithful in that which is another man's, who shall give you that which is your own?

Luke 16:10–12

"I like work; it fascinates me. I can sit and look at it for hours," insists humorist Jerome K. Jerome. Unfortunately, many others, although not exactly fascinated by their work, can make it last as long as necessary to avoid whatever it is they don't really want to do.

In early 1987, M. David Lowe Personnel Agency surveyed two hundred Houston workers. They asked about the workers' New Year's resolutions concerning their job. The third most frequently given answer was, "Not waste as much time," which ranked right after "Learning more about the company and industry operations" and "Learning more about computers." Resolution number four fell along the same lines of productivity: "Don't be late."

Anyone who's been in the work force long knows the kind of wasted, nonproductive time these respondents were guiltily referring to. Employees call in sick when the weather's too bad to get out of the house; then they call in sick when the weather's too pretty to waste inside an office building. They arrive late when they oversleep, and they arrive late when they get no sleep.

But tardiness and absenteeism are only a small part of the problem. Once they get to their desks, according to productivity experts, most office employees waste at least 45 percent of the day. A 1983 study of nonmanagerial employees conducted by Daniel Yankelovich's Public Agenda Foundation revealed that only 22 percent of the employees say they work at full potential. Nearly one-half (44 percent) admit that they

218

expend the minimum effort to get by on their job. Three out of four workers say they could do more work, if they wanted to (*Training and Development Journal*, April 1987). The Robert Half consulting firm estimates that theft of productive time costs the American economy $170 billion annually (*Wall Street Journal*, May 13, 1987).

Ask many of these unproductive people if they put in an honest day's work, and they will answer, "No, but. . . ." The reasons are varied:

- "Everybody does it. They expect it."
- "At work is the only time I have."
- "You should see what my boss gets away with."
- "But this job is so boring. If I didn't spend a little time socializing, I'd go nuts."
- "Have you ever seen my paycheck? I'm not going to bust my gut for that little dribble."
- "I'm an unorganized person. That's just the way I am."

Whatever their excuses or reasons, employees would probably become more productive if they really took to heart the scriptural admonitions about productivity.

Thomas Edison said of his great accomplishments, "I never did anything worth doing by accident, nor did any of my inventions come by accident; they came by work." Lack of talent or know-how is seldom the productivity problem.

Instead, the problem is no harder or no easier than a complete change of attitude. The proper attitude could even change the legitimate responses about lack of productivity, such as a lack of time-management skills. If a person were committed to improving those skills, there are self-help books, magazine articles, and seminars available to him on every hand.

To bring on that change of attitude, we should first try simple cheerfulness. Cheerfulness gives great strength. During the recent depression in the oil industry, I commented to a manager about the attitude of his employees. "I guess that since so many people are being laid off these days, your employees are just grateful to still be working. I suppose you see an improvement in attitude and increased productivity in their efforts to keep their jobs."

He shook his head and replied grimly, "Just the opposite. Everybody has a grudge. They don't get anything done for sitting around and grousing about how bad it's going to get."

When we feel sullen or irritable, we're sapping our own energy. A smile, a perky step, and a sense of gratefulness invigorates our bodies.

Perhaps we should also try improving the way we spend our time off the job. According to minister and educator Charles R. Brown, "We have too many people who live without working, and we have altogether too many who work without living." Not being machines, we can't, of course, turn our minds on and off as we would the light switch when we enter the workplace.

But some of us live such dull, meaningless lives off the job that we come to work to play. That is, we cultivate no outside interests or friends and find that our only source of interaction with others is between eight and five. When we play hard after hours, we also feel like working hard on the job.

Finally, to improve our attitude about productivity, we need to try putting ourselves on the other side of the fence. That is, we should put ourselves in the place of our customer or boss. Do we respond to customers and clients as we would like to be treated? Are we as helpful as we could be in the situation, or do most of our conversations end like this: "That's not my area of responsibility. I don't know who you need to talk to, but it's not me."

How would we, as bosses, feel signing our own paycheck? Would we be eager to pay someone our salary for the work we do? Business owners insist that it's not easy to find employees who "work as to the Lord." A mechanic recently explained to me why he had not hired any help and was instead turning away business. "We didn't get any more done when I used to have someone else helping me, because I then found I had to spend my time standing behind the guy as he put the car door back on, begging him to do it right."

Charles M. Schwab, steel magnate, concluded: "The man who does not work for the love of work but only for money is not likely to make money nor to find much fun in life."

I think most employees will agree that those who never do any more than they get paid for, never get paid for more than they do.

To put it bluntly, we say money talks. We pay sales commissions that are directly derived from one's effort. Those who are productive and suited to their jobs seek out those situations; those who are less productive and unsuited to their jobs want to be paid regardless of the results.

Scripture mentions an even stronger link than the one between money and productivity; the relationship between God and productivity. A higher motivation for the Christian is to work "as to the Lord" (Colossians 3:23). When is the last time you worked nine to five with the awareness that God was looking over your shoulder? If we did that, we might all take on a new perspective about productivity.

For Further Reflection:

And whatsoever ye do in word or deed, do all in the name of the Lord Jesus, giving thanks to God and the Father by him.

Colossians 3:17

Servants, obey in all things your masters according to the flesh; not with eyeservice, as menpleasers; but in single-ness of heart, fearing God: And whatsoever ye do, do it heartily, as to the Lord, and not unto men; Knowing that of the Lord ye shall receive the reward of the inheritance: for ye serve the Lord Christ.

Colossians 3:22–24

First Thing Monday Morning

The soul of the sluggard craves, and gets nothing, while the soul of the diligent is richly supplied.

Proverbs 13:4 RSV

A faithful employee is as refreshing as a cool day in the hot summertime.

Proverbs 25:13 TLB

46. Keeping the Sabbath and Your Sanity

Remember the sabbath day, to keep it holy. Six days shalt thou labour, and do all thy work.

Exodus 20:8, 9

If you keep the Sabbath holy, not having your own fun and business on that day, but enjoying the Sabbath and speaking of it with delight as the Lord's holy day, and honoring the Lord in what you do, not following your own desires and pleasure, nor talking idly—then the Lord will be your delight, and I will see to it that you ride high, and get your full share of the blessings I promised to Jacob, your father. The Lord has spoken.

Isaiah 58:13,14 TLB

". . . For the Son of man is lord of the sabbath." And he went on from there, and entered their synagogue.

223

And behold, there was a man with a withered hand.
And they asked him, "Is it lawful to heal on the
sabbath?" so that they might accuse him. He said to
them, "What man of you, if he has one sheep and it
falls into a pit on the sabbath, will not lay hold of it
and lift it out? Of how much more value is a man
than a sheep! So it is lawful to do good on the
sabbath."

Matthew 12:8–12 RSV

Richard Magnussen, CEO of an Ontario furniture manufacturing company, had to answer a tough question from
one of his managers. The employee had noticed that he
seemed to put a lot of emphasis on his relationship to
God and had expressed a desire to run his business on
biblical principles. But the manager persisted about his
puzzlement. "If you're following biblical principles around
here, then why do we participate in trade shows on
Sunday?"

Taken back by the apparent inconsistency, Richard
didn't have an answer for his employee. Instead, he went
home to think things over. Year after year, his company
had participated in the four annual trade exhibits at
which most of the year's business was generated. He
thought back to his beginnings, when his company was
doing only $29,000 in annual sales. Since that beginning,
he'd become much more aware of God's claim on his
life and had become a deacon, a community leader, and
even a Saturday seminar leader on biblical business principles.

But Richard still had no answer for the manager who
asked why he opened his trade booth on Sunday. The only
conclusion he could come to, after much prayer, was that he
shouldn't open. Although not legalistic about Sunday obser-

vance, he regretted putting his employees in a position of having to work rather than worship on that day.

So, even with the industry in a slump and fearing a big financial loss because 70 percent of their orders were always written on Sundays, Richard hung a closed sign on his trade-show booth. The sign simply stated that because he wanted to keep the Lord's Day holy, he could not open for business that day. He apologized for the inconvenience and asked retailers to please stop by again on Monday.

To his surprise, they did. A long line waited as he approached his exhibit on Monday morning. As one of his customers told him, "I don't agree with your ideas, but I respect a man of integrity. That's the kind of man I want to do business with." On that first Monday after the Sunday closing, his company wrote over 30 percent more orders than usual for that day. Within months of that trade show, his furniture was back-ordered nine months, and he had to build a new manufacturing plant. The company paid cash for the plant!

The following year, a survey of Canadian companies based on gross profit per dollar listed the second-place company as having a 10 percent profit on the dollar. Richard's company came in first place, with a 30 percent profit on the dollar.

God honors those who honor Him.

We create our own messes when we *don't* honor Him. A friend of mine phoned to say that she wouldn't see me in Bible study on Sunday morning because she and her husband had some work that simply had to be done on a new software package he was developing for the gas industry. The following Sunday, when she returned to church, I asked her how her week had gone. She smiled sheepishly. "Not too good. We spent from Monday until Thursday trying to get ourselves out of the mess that we made last Sunday."

So why do we have God's command to keep His day holy? For one thing, He knew we needed the rest. A pastor friend of mine used to say that you could take your Sundays one day at a time, or you could take them all at once in the hospital. Stress-management experts are confirming what God knew all along: Our bodies and minds need time to lie fallow for a while each week, so that we can be productive when we do work.

But as theologian David Swing points out, "Rest is valuable only so far as it is a contrast. Pursued as an end, it becomes a most pitiable condition." The Lord's Day is also for doing good.

Observing a list of *don't*s, as the Pharisees did, is always easier than observing a list of *do*s. But Jesus said that He came not to destroy the law, but to add to it. His additional interpretation that the Lord's Day was meant for our use in doing good gives a positive, active twist to the earlier commandment. How often do we go one step further than rest and actually do good things for others on Sundays?

Finally, Sundays are for thought, for reflection on God and His will for our lives and businesses. To many people, time for thought is time for guilt, emptiness, even pain. Nineteenth-century lawyer and financier Owen D. Young observed: "Leisure is pain; take off our chariot wheels and how heavily we drag the load of life. It is our curse, like that of Cain; it makes us wander earth around to fly that tyrant, thought."

If Sundays bring such emptiness that we need our work to mask it, we should immediately investigate further. What else in our life needs attention to bring us into a right relationship with God?

Sorting our Sundays from the other six days while assembling ourselves with other believers to worship is a good place to start.

For Further Reflection:

Ye shall keep my sabbaths, and reverence my sanctuary: I am the Lord.

Leviticus 19:30

Keeping the Sabbath and Your Sanity

Keep the sabbath day to sanctify it, as the Lord thy God hath commanded thee.

Deuteronomy 5:12

Not forsaking the assembling of ourselves together, as the manner of some is; but exhorting one another: and so much the more, as ye see the day approaching.

Hebrews 10:25

47. Sales Techniques
From the Apostle Paul

But I do not account my life of any value nor as precious to myself, if only I may accomplish my course and the ministry which I received from the Lord Jesus, to testify to the gospel of the grace of God. . . . Therefore I testify to you this day that I am innocent of the blood of all of you, for I did not shrink from declaring to you the whole counsel of God.

Acts 20:24, 26, 27 RSV

Few salespeople are as sold on their company, their product, or their career goals as the Apostle Paul was on his mission in life. That's understandable, of course; Paul's goals were far more worthy than any such earthly pursuits. Nevertheless, most of us can pick up a few pointers from his persuasive manner and apply them to our own business efforts.

First of all, Paul kept people foremost in his mind. They

were important to him, and he remembered their names. In chapter sixteen of his letter to the Romans, he called thirty-two people by name in passing on his greetings to them! Did you ever wonder why he didn't just say, "Tell everybody hello"? People's names are music to their ears. When you call someone by name, you single him out from the crowd and assure him that he is individually special to you.

Yet, how many times do we receive thank-you or congratulatory memos in the office addressed "To all department personnel"? Such a blanket reference defeats the purpose of the whole commendation. How many sales letters have you received that take four paragraphs to tell you all about the writer's company and only one paragraph to discuss your needs, as the customer?

Persuasive people remember names and treat individuals to the attention they deserve. They focus their attention on the co-worker's or customer's needs and interests.

Second, Paul started on common ground with his listeners, taking a positive rather than a negative tone. In his address on Mars Hill, he began with a compliment: "Men of Athens, I perceive that in every way you are very religious" (Acts 17:22 RSV). A little later in that same address, he agreed with and quoted one of their own poets about the nature of God: "In him we live and move and have our being" (Acts 17:28 RSV). These people were capable, Paul implied, of deep thought and intellectual pursuits, needing only to explore their ideas to discover ultimate and complete truth.

Later, in his defense before Governor Felix, he expressed a positive, complimentary attitude about his judge's experience: "Realizing that for many years you have been judge over this nation, I cheerfully make my defense" (Acts 24:10 RSV).

In other words, on both these occasions, Paul did not imply that his listeners were unenlightened fools, but rather that they were intelligent people who would make the right decisions, if given all the alternatives.

Many people in a sales situation, particularly those sitting around a conference table with clients or co-workers, cast their positive good ideas in a negative shadow: "Listen, I've got a better way to do that. You're spending about fifty percent more time on that project than necessary." Such a negative comment isn't nearly as persuasive and readily accepted as, "Would you be interested in an idea that I think can increase your productivity by fifty percent?"

Persuasive people are careful about how they word their suggestions or sales pitch, so their listeners don't feel put down before accepting what they say or doing what they suggest.

A third important aspect of Paul's effectiveness was his sincerity. "I always take pains to have a clear conscience toward God and toward men" (Acts 24:16 RSV). That belief in the truth of what he preached came primarily from personal experience. His defense before his own Jewish brothers (Acts 22) rang with the sincerity of his convictions because of the changes in his own life—his thinking, his attitude, his behavior, his goals.

Have you ever wondered how much more effective TV testimonials would be if the viewer knew the celebrity wasn't being paid to tout the product? If we knew William (the Refrigerator) Perry really ate Burger King hamburgers? If we knew James Coburn really "mastered the possibilities with MasterCard"?

Although advertisers know that big-name testimonials sell products, they would agree that all the paid commercials in the world aren't nearly as persuasive as one candid shot of the President of the United States or America's favorite pro football quarterback using their product or service.

Sincerity counts. In the conference room, at the podium, in the classroom. Listeners even react to sincerity over the phone lines; callers who sound like they're reading a planned script are often answered with a click and a dial tone.

No matter that it's a cliché, persuasive people practice what they preach.

Fourth, Paul was challenged, not overcome, by obstacles. Acts 20 and 2 Corinthians 11 give long lists of afflictions and obstacles Paul overcame to keep on persuading people of the truth of the Gospel. Will any rejection that modern-day salespeople suffer ever measure up to the things Paul experienced?

When discouraged, persuasive people should not ask, "Will I feel rejected?" Rather, they should ask, "Will this no ruin my life? Will it cost my loss of self-respect?" Usually, neither is the case.

When the feared outcome is not so devastating, persuasive people are much more willing to continue the process with continued hope for success.

Some salespeople adopt the "win some, lose some" philosophy much too easily. That is, when someone raises an objection or even a question about their idea, they tend to give up the selling effort, rather than put in a little more thought, investigate that objection, and come up with an appropriate response. No one ever claimed being persuasive was easy. Persuasive people think obstacles are worth hurdling.

Finally, Paul, as a good salesperson, asked for the order. That is, he didn't leave his listeners comfortably contemplating their next move; he called them to decisive action.

To a lame man hearing him preach at Lystra, he said, "Stand upright on your feet." The man stood and walked. To the Philippian jailer, he answered, "Believe in the Lord Jesus, and you will be saved, you and your household." To the Jews plotting to kill him, he demanded a trial before Caesar.

Persuasive people follow through with their ideas, products, or services by helping listeners put their words into actions—whether it's signing a check, approving a proce-dure or policy, joining a cause, or expressing faith.

In all areas of life where they are called on to be per-suasive—with families, co-workers, clients, or fellow Christians—persuasive people:

- Make people feel good about themselves, whether it's by remembering their name or their hobby or their wishes.
- Start where others are, at their level of understanding and with what they perceive as their need.
- Believe in their answer to the problem or situation, and show that confidence or belief by their own attitude and behavior.
- Make the extra effort to hurdle objections and obstacles.
- Ask for action and results, not simply leave listeners com-placently contemplating.

Take a few minutes to think of areas of your life where you'd like to be more persuasive. Why not rethink your approach and make the necessary changes in your wording, your attitude, and your action?

For Further Reflection:

And whatsoever ye do, do it heartily, as to the Lord, and not unto men.

Colossians 3:23

48. Speaking of Speaking Skills

From a wise mind comes careful and persuasive speech.

Proverbs 16:23 TLB

Let your speech be alway with grace, seasoned with salt, that ye may know how ye ought to answer every man.

Colossians 4:6

But sanctify the Lord God in your hearts: and be ready always to give an answer to every man that asketh you a reason of the hope that is in you with meekness and fear.

1 Peter 3:15

In his book *People and Performance,* management guru Peter Drucker observes:

233

The further away your job is from manual work, the larger the organization of which you are an employee, the more important it will be that you know how to convey your thoughts in writing or speaking. In the very large organization, whether it is the government, the large business corporation, or the Army, this ability to express yourself is perhaps the most important of all skills you can possess.

The Apostle Paul certainly exemplified one who was always ready and capable of expressing himself about his faith. No doubt all the disciples, regardless of their education, became capable of expressing themselves, their faith, and Christ's mission. Moses, too, realized the importance of being able to speak well in order to lead the Israelites out of Egypt. That's why he complained about his stumbling speech until God sent along his brother, Aaron, as spokesman.

"But," some employees may counter, "I'm not the leader of a nation, like Moses, or a corporation executive." Again, Jesus gave no outs because of a lowly position. You recall the blind man whom Jesus healed on the Sabbath, to the chagrin of the Pharisees? What was the parents' response to the authorities about the circumstances of his healing? "He is of age. Go ask him" (*see* John 9). At some time or another, we all will find it beneficial, even necessary, to be able to express ourselves well.

We never know when we will be called on to represent our God or our company or God in our company. We, as employers and employees, have to be ready to give an answer to everyone who asks who we are, what we're about, and how we can help our fellowman.

As Christians, our speaking, as well as our living, should be above the norm. With study, motivation, practice, and attention to the examples of others, we can avoid becoming one of the following varieties of corporate speakers we've all heard:

Guru: He knows his subject and spouts off in vague, complex language, trying to impress rather than to express. He acts bored with the whole occasion and in turn bores everyone else beyond their need or interest.

Showman: He is an egotist who likes being in front of people, no matter what the subject. He jokes, ad-libs, pokes fun, puts on a show, and says nothing of value. He wastes his audience's time.

Shrink-wrapped Package: He knows what he knows and doesn't care if he communicates that knowledge to his audience. The audience's needs are of no interest to him. He establishes no rapport, and people just can't "touch" him. He uses vague, complex language, trying to impress rather than express.

Christian speakers should give more effort to the occasion—whether it's to present a product to a customer, to present a problem to senior management, or to present one's faith to a nonbeliever.

Hal Persons, a colleague of mine from New York, works among such corporations as AT&T, Chase Manhattan Bank, and IBM, teaching their executives how to make oral presentations. Hal insists that all of us have the ability to express ourselves adequately one-on-one or before a group. We grow up speaking naturally, with little effort. Only when we get into the school system do we learn to fear speaking before a group.

If we learn fear, we can also unlearn it.

The first step toward becoming a good spokesperson is simply to be the natural person that God created. When our love, concern, and enthusiasm for our subject and the other person come through, God will bless the results. The following tips, gained from innumerable well-known speakers, will enable you to answer nonbelievers about the hope and faith within you, and will also make you a more valuable employee to your organizationn.

Arouse interest in your subject.

Plan your speeches, if possible.

State your objectives up front. Giving your audience the big picture first will help them understand the details as you proceed.

Get your audience to participate with you in considering your subject. Can you ask a question? Ask them to write their objectives, problems, or solutions? Ask for an opinion?

Adapt your words to the listeners' needs. If your listeners are lawyers, assure them that your pens are perfect for signing documents. If your listeners are salesclerks, explain that your pens come with chains, so they can't be detached from the cash register.

Use the "you and I" perspective. Be direct and approachable with your audience.

Do not try to *impress* with big words and long sentences. Instead, aim to *express*. Use clear, understandable terms; as a result, you will impress your listeners with your ideas.

Overcome language or education barriers by using clear, concrete, visual terms. Why say *monetary constraints* when you mean *budget*? Why say *to enhance personal productivity* when you mean *to help you type faster*?

Use analogies, experience, or history to make your topic easier to understand and evaluate.

Use frequent pauses, to let your listeners process what you have said.

Provide a focus as you talk, such as a visual, if possible. This visual helps you to plan what you want to say and helps your listeners remember what you have said.

Do not react defensively to questions. Restate the question, to make sure you have heard correctly. Organize your answer explicitly for the question. Then verify that you have answered to the listener's satisfaction. Do not return a hostile answer for a hostile question; you'll lose your audience.

Use humor. Be able to laugh at your own mistakes. Such

vulnerability helps listeners identify with you and wish you well.

Do not plan your gestures. Be spontaneous and normal, with a delivery style that results from enthusiasm, confidence in your knowledge of the subject, and a lack of nervousness because of your integrity.

Read the body language of your listeners. Are they growing weary? Are they losing interest? Do they look puzzled? Meet their needs immediately.

Be considerate of your audience's time. Jesus and the apostles spoke for hours on eternally important subjects; taper your own talks accordingly.

Be real and genuine. Be willing to show your emotional attachment to and enthusiasm for your topic.

Remember that your words will not hide egotism, hypocrisy, boredom, lack of integrity, lack of emotional involvement, or any prejudice. Never be at a loss for words when you have an opportunity to explain your product, your service, or your faith on the job.

For Further Reflection:

A good man out of the good treasure of the heart bringeth forth good things: and an evil man out of the evil treasure bringeth forth evil things. But I say unto you, That every idle word that men shall speak, they shall give account thereof in the day of judgment. For by thy words thou shalt be justified, and by thy words thou shalt be condemned.

Matthew 12:35–37

49. When a Fulfilling Job Leaves You Unfulfilled

. . . I am come that they might have life, and that they might have it more abundantly.

John 10:10

When thou hast eaten and art full, then thou shalt bless the Lord thy God for the good land which he hath given thee. Beware that thou forget not the Lord thy God, in not keeping his commandments, and his judgments, and his statutes, which I command thee this day: Lest when thou hast eaten and art full, and hast built goodly houses, and dwelt therein; And when thy herds and thy flocks multiply, and thy silver and thy gold is multiplied, and all that thou hast is multiplied; Then thine heart be lifted up, and thou forget the Lord thy God, which brought thee forth out of the land of Egypt, from the house of bondage. . . . And thou say in thine heart, My power and the might of mine hand hath gotten me this wealth.

Deuteronomy 8:10–14, 17

Commit your work to the Lord, then it will succeed.

Proverbs 16:3 TLB

Try this pop quiz:

- Name the five most successful individuals in the United States.
- When you introduce acquaintances to each other, do you identify them by mentioning what they do for a living, or where they live, or something they've accomplished?
- Have you spent more of your waking hours this past year on reaching spiritual goals or business goals?
- Have you spent more time this past year balancing your checkbook or teaching your children Scripture principles?
- How many times did you choose spending time with your family or friends over spending time at work? Spending time on a work project over family and friends?
- Where did you spend the most money? On charitable projects, including your tithes and offerings to God, or on your own leisure, holidays, and vacations?

Now, consider your answers. Did money and status dictate your answers to numbers one and two? Is money the biggest determiner in your choices about time and relationships? Usually, we are better at defining success than living it.

Ambition, the spark of financial success, is the fire that ignites creativity, intelligence, and energy when enthusiasm has burned itself out, and the flame of ambition can't be lit by anyone other than its owner. But, unlike ambition's beginning, many things can be responsible for putting out its spark.

Often, the most common extinguisher of ambition is success. Show me a person who owns every material possession, has accomplished every goal she once had, and is acclaimed by friends and strangers alike for her accomplishments, and I'll show you a person who has extinguished her ambition for the world's definition of success. That person comes to ask, "Is this all there is?"

Often that drive to excel is restlessness. Even God rested on the seventh day—not from physical exhaustion, but from a sense of satisfaction, of meaningful pause. He summed up: "It is good."

Therein lies the difference: Successful people often miss the feeling of satisfaction—they do not feel happy—because what they've done is not meaningful, is not attached to a worthwhile cause or result.

No one can read the Bible and sincerely doubt that God intends us to lead successful lives; the difference of opinion comes in how we define success.

Undoubtedly, if I took a reader poll and asked you to mail in a response card with your definition of success, I would get a pile of comments such as: "Pleasing God with my life"; "Having a successful marriage and well-adjusted children"; "Being happy"; "Doing what I enjoy."

But do you really, really feel that way? Does your daily practice show that to be your real conviction? "Singleness of purpose," said John D. Rockefeller, Jr., "is one of the chief essentials for success in life, no matter what may be one's aim."

While my company was recently in New York exhibiting for a trade show, I dropped by to visit my literary agent. After we had discussed a rejection of my latest book proposal and a near-miss subrights video sale, he asked me how the trade show had gone. Growing more animated, I began to tell him about various corporation reps coming by my booth, about an overseas assignment, and about a few invitations to speak at conventions. My agent dropped his pencil in mid-sentence and asked, "Then why in the world are you writing books? Why don't you stop this nonsense and make some money?"

Although I only smiled at the age-old questions writers ask themselves and one another, I knew the answer: satisfaction.

But that answer isn't easily arrived at. For me or for you, I don't think. It usually takes a close glimpse of death.

A family doctor once counseled a teenage girl who had attempted suicide: "You know," he said, "you could have made your parents and your friends really sad today. They would have cried a lot. But after a while, your mom and dad would have had to go back to work; your friends would have gone on to school. They would be forced to go on with life without you, to forget you."

I think it's this aspect of death that scares most of us, rather than the actual physical dying. We will have lived, and yet, after we're gone, everything will be the same; our life will not have mattered.

What gives life meaning is not what we accomplish on the job. It is not what we own. It is not whom we know. It is not who praises us. What gives life meaning is attaching ourselves to something that is significant, to something meaningful. That means linking our lives with God and His purpose in the world. When we do, we'll find that happiness and fulfillment have slipped inside us when we weren't looking.

I like the admonition of Albert Einstein: "Try not to become a man of success but rather try to become a man of value."

For Further Reflection:

He who gives heed to the word will prosper, and happy is he who trusts in the Lord.

Proverbs 16:20 RSV

First Thing Monday Morning

Beloved, I wish above all things that thou mayest prosper and be in health, even as thy soul prospereth.

3 John 2

He that trusteth in his riches shall fall: but the righteous shall flourish as a branch.

Proverbs 11:28

Wickedness never brings real success; only the godly have that.

Proverbs 12:3 TLB

50. Where Was Solomon When I Needed Wisdom?

If any of you lack wisdom, let him ask of God, that giveth to all men liberally, and upbraideth not; and it shall be given him.

James 1:5

Wisdom gives: A long, good life, riches, honor, pleasure, peace.

Proverbs 3:16, 17 TLB

Trust in the Lord with all thine heart; and lean not unto thine own understanding. In all thy ways acknowledge him, and he shall direct thy paths.

Proverbs 3:5, 6

"Why do we always find things the last place we look?" the riddle goes. Answer: Because when we find it, we stop looking. An equally puzzling question: "Why do we take all our decisions to God last, rather than first?"

Most of us still get our wisdom through an ineffective, outdated method: Experience. We find a lot of things that don't work, while we waste time, money, and effort in the process.

First, we look for facts. But the problem no longer is not having enough information to conduct our business. Rather, it is that we have too much information. With our modern technology, we have access to databases on every conceivable subject and enough computer printouts to wrap the world several times. Knowledge and facts we have.

What we lack is the understanding to *use* the information we have. Proverbs 2:6 says that wisdom encompasses both knowledge and the understanding and proper application of that knowledge. In "computerese," wisdom is an analysis of the printout in terms of recommendations.

When the facts don't give us the answers we need, some of us look to the experience of our older colleagues and our bosses. *Mentoring*, the buzzword of the fast trackers in the early eighties, meant latching onto a gray-haired God substitute who could introduce us to the right people, advise us of the experience we needed, and, if we were lucky, could create the correct circumstances for our promotion.

But with our more experienced colleagues, just as with the computer and our latest technology, we seldom find all the wisdom we need. Even before mentoring came and went, Henry L. Mencken observed: "The older I grow the more I distrust the familiar doctrine that age brings wisdom."

Some of us look to persuasive advice givers for our wisdom. While the talkative among us are always ready to give us a piece of their mind, they often speak from little understanding. According to Sophocles, "Much wisdom often goes with fewest words."

At last, when all other sources fail and with a trail of wasted dollars and time, in desperation we find ourselves turning to God for wisdom on the job.

Nevertheless, we're welcomed whenever we get there. Our first step toward gaining God's wisdom is to know what we do not know, that is, to be aware of our shortcomings. The Apostle Paul, in 1 Corinthians 2, assured the church members of Corinth that he hadn't dared show up to preach among them armed only with his own glowing wit and wisdom. In fact, he feared and trembled with awareness of his own shortcomings. The method, as well as the results there, was God's effort. Therefore, because it was God's wisdom he shared, he had every confidence that the effects of his visit would last.

We, too, have to come to the realization that all the print-outs in the world, all the marketing plans by the best corporate planning departments, and all the technical experts available do not have all the answers. Saying that we recognize these limitations is one thing; believing it, is something else again.

A second condition of wisdom is to acknowledge God as the true Source and to ask for His guidance. God doesn't force His wisdom on us, but James 1:5 assures us that He gives liberally when we acknowledge our need and His supply.

A third condition of wisdom is to live righteously with the knowledge and wisdom we have. God gives answers to those whom He can trust to use them for His glory and the benefit of mankind. We can rest assured that God won't give us the wisdom to design and submit a client proposal that will lead us into swindling our suppliers.

A fourth condition and advantage in finding wisdom is that we walk with wise men. God's wisdom often comes via other believers. If we hang out with fools, we shouldn't be surprised at their foolish advice. In fact, we'll often have trouble separating it from the wisdom of God's messengers.

So how do we know whether our wisdom is from God, or if it's simply the product of jumping on our colleagues' bandwagon, riding a promising wave of the future, or using good old uncommon sense?

Perhaps the following observations will help.

God's wisdom makes a man compete only with himself—to increase his wisdom. The world's wisdom encourages us to compete with others.

God's wisdom makes us straightforward. The world's wisdom promotes deceit and manipulation.

God's wisdom leads to harmony. The world's wisdom generates disagreement, anger, and conflict.

God's wisdom treats all human beings with respect. The world's wisdom shows partiality, rewarding only those who have something to give in return.

God's wisdom will lead to kindness. The world's wisdom will lead to mean-spiritedness and even cruelty.

God's wisdom humbles us when we learn of our shortcomings. The world's wisdom makes us proud when we learn of the shortcomings of others.

God's wisdom encourages us to set personal goals and move toward them. The world's wisdom tells us to be complacent with what we are.

God's wisdom brings happiness when we achieve what He wants in our life. The world's wisdom makes us happy when we win praise from our colleagues.

God's wisdom will direct us toward holy, moral actions. The world's wisdom will direct us toward what is expedient.

God's wisdom will result in long-term success. The world's wisdom will result in only short-term profits.

True wisdom is worth the wait. But the next time you need direction in your job, get genuine wisdom in the first place (not the last place) you look.

For Further Reflection:

He who loves wisdom loves his own best interest and will be a success.

Proverbs 19:8 TLB

Where Was Solomon When I Needed Wisdom?

Determination to be wise is the first step toward becoming wise! And with your wisdom, develop common sense and good judgment.

Proverbs 4:7 TLB

For wisdom is better than rubies; and all the things that may be desired are not to be compared to it.

Proverbs 8:11

My son, keep sound wisdom and discretion; let them not escape from your sight, and they will be life for your soul and adornment for your neck. Then you will walk on your way securely and your foot will not stumble.

Proverbs 3:21–23 RSV

He that is void of wisdom despiseth his neighbour: but a man of understanding holdeth his peace.

Proverbs 11:12

A wise man is strong; yea, a man of knowledge increaseth strength.

Proverbs 24:5

51. Worship Nine to Five

My mouth is filled with thy praise, and with thy glory all the day.

Psalms 71:8 RSV

But his delight is in the law of the Lord; and in his law doth he meditate day and night.

Psalms 1:2

My mouth will tell of thy righteous acts, of thy deeds of salvation all the day, for their number is past my knowledge.

Psalms 71:15 RSV

"Morning, George."
"Good morning."
"How's it going, Carol?"
"Okay. How about you?"
"Hello."

And so it goes around most offices at the beginning of each day. Yet those who would never think of stumbling into work without speaking to their colleagues often pass the whole day without speaking to God. It's not that we need to make *our* presence known to God, as we do to our co-workers; it's that we need to acknowledge *His* presence in our lives.

Not to downplay the importance of corporate worship with other believers, but private worship outside the walls of the church building is most meaningful. Often, the more formal our worship is, the more ritualistic it is. That is, we can rise, sit, stand, sing, and pray on cue in our churches without ever personally "making connection" with God. If we're not careful, we fall into the habit of letting the ritual substitute for the real.

Therefore, those private, spontaneous moments of worship between 9:00 and 5:00, Monday through Friday, can be as meaningful, if not more so, than formal worship in changing our behavior and attitudes on the job.

These worship experiences may be planned or unplanned. Like several other firms founded by Christians, a group of senior executives at the headquarters of Stewart Title Guaranty Company meet before work hours every day for Bible study and prayer together. As an outgrowth of that time, their worship has set the atmosphere for the entire office.

While conducting a writing seminar there, on one occasion I chatted with a secretary before class. Not having met me before, she confided what she thought was a secret. "Let me tell you something about this company before you get too involved here. Things are really . . . different. Some of these people meet every morning to read the Bible and things like that. They even meet to pray over decisions, sometimes. You'll see—it really sets a weird atmosphere around here—affects policies, things like that."

Although her tone and facial expression conveyed her comments negatively, the effect of this group's worship was the same; it was a witness of their faith. And that witness is ongoing. Four years later, in an interview with a *Wall Street Journal* reporter, I mentioned CEO Carloss Morris at Stewart Title. The reporter commented, "I think I've heard of him several places around town. Isn't he that religious guy that runs his business by the Bible or something?"

Others, like Carloss Morris, use the workplace for worship and witness. Speaking at a Chamber of Commerce marketing seminar, Ninfa Laurenzo, sixty-two-year-old owner of nine very successful Mexican restaurants in Houston and Dallas, assured the audience that her marketing plan could be summed up simply: Love God, and love the customer. When pushed further for explanation of her success, she expanded, "I love God with all my heart and all my soul. It can't help but spill over to my customers. They know it."

But even more than the witness our worship gives and more than the tone it sets for our office, worship feeds our own spirit.

What better place, what more hectic place, do we go where we need renewed strength and rest than the office? Isaiah 40:31 promises renewed strength—both physical and emotional. A friend of mine recently related to me how her private worship got her through each day during marital difficulties:

"Some days I'd go to the office and force myself to try to concentrate on the job. But about half a day was all I could stand. At lunch, I'd get out my New Testament and walk down to the park near our office and just sit and read and listen and think. If it hadn't been for those times, for that midday lift, for knowing God was there, I think I would not have been able to work during those months."

Like my friend, I, too, have experienced those unplanned moments of worship when circumstances on the job made me so aware of God's care and provision that I couldn't help but immediately stop what I was doing and offer praise.

Not so long ago, I was facing a difficult circumstance in my own life, needing to be off work for an extended period of time. As I called clients and tried to rearrange project-due dates, it began to look as though things weren't going to work out, and that I might lose several thousand dollars due to clients' cancellations. But as I lifted my mind to God that afternoon and asked Him to take over the situation, things began to turn around. Two hours and several phone calls later, not only had I held onto the former projects, I had accumulated three more requests for our services, to be rendered on my own timetable.

Was I in a worshipful spirit? You bet! I gathered my husband and both kids around to explain what God had just pulled off!

Yes, spontaneous worship, whenever it happens—and particularly on the job—can be as meaningful nine to five Monday through Friday, as Sunday morning between ten and noon.

God is ready when you are.

For Further Reflection:

And my tongue will talk of thy righteous help all the day long, for they have been put to shame and disgraced who sought to do me hurt.

Psalms 71:24 RSV

By him therefore let us offer the sacrifice of praise to God continually, that is, the fruit of our lips giving thanks to his name.

Hebrews 13:15

God is a Spirit: and they that worship him must worship him in spirit and in truth.

John 4:24

52. You Can Count on Me: Unless the Other Guy Gets the Ten Talents

---

Moreover it is required in stewards, that a man be found faithful.

1 Corinthians 4:2

So take the talent from him, and give it to him who has the ten talents. For to every one who has will more be given, and he will have abundance; but from him who has not, even what he has will be taken away.

Matthew 25:28, 29 RSV

Having gifts that differ according to the grace given to us, let us use them: if prophecy, in proportion to our faith; if service, in our serving; he who teaches, in his teaching; he who exhorts, in his exhortation; he who contributes, in liberality; he who gives aid,

with zeal; he who does acts of mercy, with cheerfulness.

Romans 12:6–8 RSV

One of my friends, a former flight attendant, has seen talent and potential thwarted quite dramatically in a colleague's life. My friend and her colleague Donna flew together in their early twenties, and Donna shared the deepest longing and disappointment of her life. All during her childhood, she had desperately wanted to study piano and violin, but her mother refused to hear of the idea. To be a musician, according to her mother, was to waste her life in pursuit of a financially unrewarding endeavor.

In her adult years, the childhood longing to become a world-famous musician became an obsession with Donna. She had begun piano and violin lessons on her own, but felt that it was too late to achieve her goals. As a well-paid airline attendant, she lived in a luxurious apartment overlooking the lake on Chicago's Lake Shore Drive. Her rooms were filled wall to wall with expensive musical instruments, stereo systems, and classical albums and tapes. To the exclusion of all other interests, she talked intimately about all composers and concert pianists who came to Chicago to entertain, rarely missing their performances.

One day at the height of her distress about her wasted talents, she stood at her apartment window and tossed her Saks Fifth Avenue clothes and all her musical possessions into the street. She now writes letters to my friend from a mental institution, complaining about her mother's part in her wasted talents and begging for money.

Most of us cannot blame others for our failure to develop our God-given talents. We are our own worst critic and discourager.

We look around at the vice-presidents in the company, with their still-dark coiffures, their energy, their quick ability to spot a trend that becomes an $8 million line of business. We hear the eloquent speaker who is relaxed and confident before a group of fifty prospective customers who are ready to buy. We consider the engineer, frequently published in technical journals and held in high esteem by her colleagues.

In other words, we make comparisons. And those comparisons almost always hinder our own progress in developing our talents and working to our highest potential. We assume that the other person has more talent than we do and, therefore, that we missed "our fair share." We become envious and either give up or excuse ourselves for not doing the best with the abilities we do have.

Unlike the car rental agency that is in second place and tries harder, some people draw a defensive, protective shield around themselves and refuse to try at all. They work at nothing heartily. If they don't volunteer to serve on the quality-circles task force, then no one can blame them for not coming up with any cost-saving measures. If they don't do a good job of preparing a new management report, then perhaps nobody will ask them to do it the next time.

Deciding that they can never be the best, many employees settle in to become the least.

Often employees who squander their efforts and talent in a bureaucratic structure think that if they were on their own, they could develop their talent to its highest potential. But as in other situations, man's reasoning is often directly opposite to that of Scripture. The Gospel writer tells us that he who doesn't do his best for his "master" certainly won't do any better for himself.

Check out the cases you know personally. Those who develop their talents, take advantage of all learning opportunities, and give a boss their energy and best effort usually have the same success when they leave the company and go out on their own as entrepreneurs. Those, on the other hand, who were underachievers, so to speak, when they worked for someone else rarely do any better for themselves.

Employees who do not view their work as a service to God

do it unhappily and, usually, unwell—whether the profit goes in their own pockets or someone else's.

We should never let ourselves waste time in envying the abilities of others. Our only concern should be to do the best with what we've been given. Whatever it takes to learn, grow, and become proficient at our tasks, God did not give us an option about our performance. We should consider the untapped potential beneath our exterior as if God Himself would be conducting our next annual performance review.

The story is told of a woman who once rushed up to famed violinist Fritz Kreisler after a concert and cried: "I'd give my life to play as beautifully as you do."

Kreisler replied, "I did."

What kind of return is God getting on His investment of talent in you? Why?

For Further Reflection:

He that is faithful in that which is least is faithful also in much: and he that is unjust in the least is unjust also in much. If therefore ye have not been faithful in the unrighteous mammon, who will commit to your trust the true riches? And if ye have not been faithful in that which is another man's, who shall give you that which is your own?

Luke 16:10–12

. . . For unto whomsoever much is given, of him shall be much required: and to whom men have committed much, of him they will ask the more.

Luke 12:48